DYING WITH DAD

Tough Talks for Easier Endings

YVONNE CAPUTO

FIRST EDITION

ISBNs:
eBook: 978-1-989059-98-2
Paperback: 978-1-989059-97-5

Five Wishes® is a Registered Trademark of Aging with Dignity.

ABOUT THE PUBLISHER

Ingenium Books Publishing Inc. Toronto, Ontario, Canada M6P 1Z2 All rights reserved.

ingeniumbooks.com

Cover Design by Jessica Bell Designs via Ingenium Books

Praise for Dying With Dad

"...a gift to every reader that shows, in a very real and practical sense, how to take good care of the people we love the most."

Paul Malley, president, Aging with Dignity

"...a well written and compassionate nudge to get us talking with our friends and family about how we want to live our final days, how we want to die, and how they can help us do that."

C.A. Gibbs, author of *The Picture Wall: One Woman's Story of Being (His) (Her) Their Mother*

"This book will fill your heart with love and your eyes with tears as you unpack your personal thoughts on what it means to die with dignity—and the gift that it can bring to those you love most."

Stephanie Feger, author of *Color Today Pretty: An Inspirational Guide to Living a Life in Perspective*

"Yvonne Caputo brought together a kind of end-of-life Welcome-Wagon gift package of words that is going to serve me well in the way I listen to the truth of others and speak my own."

Marie Beswick-Arthur, author of *Listen for Water,* a novel about survival, redemption, and the repair of relationships.

"...practical tools to help transform a conversation about death into a tangible plan that respectfully invites the participation of our loved ones and honours their wishes in every aspect of not only dying but living as well."

Gwyn Teatro, author of the award-winning *In the Thick of It: Mastering the Art of Leading from the Middle*

Contents

In loving memory of my father, Michael, and my mother, Teddy

Introduction

When I wrote my first book, *Flying With Dad,* many readers asked—and continue to ask—questions. But not about the parts of the book central to the main point, which is about Dad's experiences as a combat navigator of B24 bombers in the years leading up to and during World War II.

No, most of the reader questions focused specifically on the chapters where I talked about walking Dad through his Five Wishes, a document that guides a conversation with family and doctors about how you want to be treated if you become seriously ill. And I've received plenty of reader questions related to the day Dad died and I stopped the paramedics from trying to resuscitate him because he had a Do Not Resuscitate order.

"How did you have the guts to talk to your father about that?"

"How were you able to let your father die when he could have been saved? Even though that's what he said he wanted, wasn't that hard?"

It was my divine paradox: I had to do something difficult to experience something beautiful.

Hearing how readers had processed these specific chapters in *Flying with Dad* got me thinking: *dying with dignity is an idea worth talking more about*. We have so little control over most things, and we certainly have little or no control (unless we take it) about death. Thinking about my own death, what would I consider to be dying with dignity? What would a good death look like for me? Was there such a thing?

In my career working in retirement communities, my colleagues and I encouraged people to have an advance directive, and I'd done this with Dad. While it's important and incredibly helpful, even it had fallen short. It wasn't until I learned about the Five Wishes® that I realized how short.

The Five Wishes®, a registered trademark of Aging with Dignity, is a practical tool that acts as a guide for important conversations with family and doctors about how you want to be treated if you or a loved one become seriously ill.

1. The person you want to make health care decisions for you if and when you can't.
2. The kind(s) of medical treatment you want or don't want if you fall seriously ill .
3. The kind of comfort you want at the end of your life.
4. How you want to be treated in order to maintain your dignity.
5. What you want others to know and remember about you, and what you'd want to share before it's too late.

Dying with Dad is not a how-to book that will walk you through the detail of completing your own Five Wishes® document. Rather, it's my personal journey getting comfortable talking about death to the dying, and how doing the Five Wishes® with my dad changed our relationship—and his end of life experience—for the better.

End of life desires are rarely decadent. Most folks who prepare their wishes have simple requests that are easily carried out. You are most folks and so am I. To be able to speak about end-of-life wishes and know that those wishes will be honored is comforting. For example, my dad's: feet first, "Amazing Grace," keep me clean, don't need anyone to speak about me at the service, would like to be remembered for Red Cross work. Simple. Humble.

When we were at the funeral home, and my brother and sister had questions, knowing Dad's five wishes alleviated the anxiety of having to make the right choices. We knew, or I knew, because I'd asked him what he wanted.

As the response to *Flying With Dad* continues to come in, so does my desire to help others feel the joy I did when Dad died. Not because he died, but because he'd received what he wanted. His death was dignified.

I've written *Dying with Dad* to help you open the door to the possibility that you can help yourself, or perhaps your loved ones, be clear about what you want as you near the conclusion of the universal destiny that awaits us all.

1

Our Universal Destiny

*E*ach of us will die. It's a fact that causes fear and trepidation to the point that people won't talk about it.

"The elephant in the room" is a widely accepted idiom. If something is embarrassing, uncomfortable, or difficult to confront, it is more likely to become the elephant in the room—that which everyone knows is there but no one acknowledges.

In many homes, death is the elephant in the room. People arrange the furniture around its mass, vacuum under its low-slung belly, and avoid its inquisitive trunk. They close their ears to its trumpeting call and avoid staring at the expanse of gray.

In the nineteenth century, people died at home. Family members took care of the body of their loved one. They washed and positioned the body, lovingly combed their loved one's hair, and chose favorite clothing. Friends and relatives would sit with the body until the coffin and grave were prepared.

Medicine and medical practice have had a great impact on death and dying. Death, now, most often happens in hospitals or nursing homes. Medical professionals take care of the living body while it is dying, and morticians take over after death. The personalized connection between the dying and their home and family is largely lost.

There are exceptions. Hospice and palliative care teams can keep medical details in mind but focus upon what the dying desire, and some services are available to support end of life conversations.

I sometimes wonder if I am an exception; as a girl I was surrounded by death. Before I was thirty, I could list seventeen family members and friends who'd passed away. Grandparents, including the grandmother who had lived with us for a time and passed when I was a sophomore in college. I remember being relieved—her health and mental health issues had burdened us as well. My mother's brother Mac died in his late fifties from a massive heart attack. He left me fifty dollars in his will to go out and have fun on him. There were other elderly relatives, too, all whose deaths fit into what I knew was the fabric of life. Other deaths, though, were like gaping tears in that fabric.

Claude, a favorite uncle, died by suicide in 1965. Hospitalized several times for mental health issues, time and again he'd be released and return to what appeared to be a normal life. He was kind and generous, befriending a boyfriend of mine who was anything but popular with my mother. He took the two of us places, and he was the one who taught me to drive. Whenever I sneak out of a rolling stop, I still hear his admonishment.

Mom called me with the news. Claude had been back in the hospital. The staff found him in a conference room. He'd dismantled the alarm and hung himself with the wires.

It was the first time I'd had to face the idea that someone would—and could—choose not to live. And it was the first time I found myself asking questions about the part that I might have played. What had I missed? What hadn't I said or done that might have helped? Claude always seemed so upbeat around me—how could he have been so sad? Why, why, why?

About two years later, his eldest son, my cousin Jimmy, died by suicide as well. He'd almost completed his PhD in mathematics and had recently introduced us to his beautiful and delightful fiancé. It seemed as if the world were his oyster. The police in North Carolina found his car near a dense forest. Inside the car was a suicide note. It took over a year for his remains to be discovered—he'd shot himself. Again, the question: why?

Then there was the murder of another cousin, Alan. He'd returned to work after a sustained medical leave. He'd been living with his parents, and on his first day back to work he didn't come home after his shift. He hadn't said that he was going out, and he hadn't called to say he was staying with friends. The New York City police called the following day. A body had been found in Central Park with no identification, no wallet, and no money. However, inside the man's pants pocket was a bottle of prescription pills. The pharmacy gave police Alan's name and address and the police went to my aunt and uncle's house to deliver the news.

These events colored my reactions to late arrivals and phone calls the rest of my life.

Candlelight dinners are an every-night tradition that started when my husband and I were first married. We wanted to make the end of the day special. We wanted it to be a time of conversation and sharing. We wanted it to soften the experiences of our day.

One evening in the dark of winter, Kirk wasn't home at his usual time. He worked in the city, and it took anywhere from an hour to an hour and a half from door to door. When two hours passed, I started to get angry. I could save the dinner, but the food would be mush. Two and a half hours passed and I started to panic.

When he finally walked through the door, I felt immediate relief that he was safe. Then, the tension gushed out of me and my eyes filled with tears. "Where were you, and why are you so late?"

"There were some last-minute things I had to take care of. The time slipped away. I don't understand why you're so upset."

The words came tumbling out of my mouth from a reservoir that I hadn't known existed.

"I was waiting for the call that something awful had happened to you. That's how it works in my life. The phone call that came that Uncle Claude had taken his life, the phone call that his son Jimmy had done the same, the call that said my cousin Alan had been murdered outside of Central Park in New York, and worst of all the call from Dad that my darling brother Mark had been in an accident and was dead."

All of the losses of people I'd held so dear had been communicated to me by the dreaded phone call—after someone was late. Each of those deaths filled me with an anger so intense that I didn't quite know I could hold. Each an incredible waste of a human life. Uncle Claude was a sweet, gentle man who made me feel special, Jimmy about to get his PhD in math, Alan picking up the pieces of his life, only to have it snuffed out. Mark, who had just been accepted into the local college music program. Those beautiful lives, the possibilities that we all took for granted of what life might have in store, gone in a heartbeat. Or, gone with the heartbeat. Silenced.

In the aftermath of each of these deaths, an overwhelming helplessness bubbled to the surface. Four special people dying in such tragic ways. What could have been done—by me or anyone else—to prevent them? Had we done everything we could? What important conversations hadn't taken place? Was there anything that would help those of us left behind process the grief that lay in the wake of those inexplicable deaths?

But the biggest question of all: why didn't we talk about the end of life before the end of life? I began to see that in not having those talks, we missed opportunities to address issues, solve problems, to forge stronger bonds with our loved ones, and reduce post-passing regret.

My father, Michael Caputo, was a B24 navigator and served during World War II. He married, started a family and, when he left the military he went into sales, continued building model aircraft, took up photography, remained in the Air Force Reserves, and later volunteered with the Red Cross. While he was held in high regard on the career front, at home he was grumpy. Like many who served in the war, my father suffered from PTSD. Only none of us knew it back then. His bark might have been worse than his bite, but it served to keep a distance between him and me, leaving me feeling a lack of closeness with my father that would follow me into adulthood and which would require therapy for me to sort out.

Our relationship changed later in life. His willingness to share his stories about his past—and my willingness to ask him about the details —brought us together. It led me to write my first book, *Flying with Dad*, which I originally thought was about detailing his life in the military and beyond. Sharing these stories strengthened our relationship. We blossomed as father and daughter. *Flying with Dad* became a story about that, too.

It was writing *Flying with Dad* that ultimately opened the door for Dad and I to be able to have meaningful conversations about his wishes for the end of his life—conversations that gave me the gift of knowing I'd helped him leave this world on his terms. How I got there, how we had that conversation, and what difference it made on the day Dad died are the foundations for this book, *Dying with Dad*. Dad's dying wasn't something that happened *to* me, or *to* Dad. I participated with him, to create for him the conditions he wanted in his final years, months, days, and hours.

All my experiences: a teacher of children, a psychotherapist, working with the elderly and those who worked with the elderly, the influence of my mother's painful passing, writing a book to honor my father's life and being with him the day of his glorious and joyful departure from this Earth, taught me the value of talking about death, and the necessity of moving it into a non-morbid category of conversation.

End-of-life discussions can be beginnings.

End-of-life discussions, when handled with loving care, can stimulate and renew relationships, reveal previously unknown treasures in the form of people's deepest desires, and restore connections between and within them.

What would be the greatest advancement of all would be that everyone would be able to speak openly—and early—about end-of-life considerations with those they trust.

For those left behind, honoring the wishes of a loved one softens the grief. It is then a gift given, and a gift received.

2

Books and Belonging

I am on my mother's lap, and we are sitting on the ugly, maroon horsehair sofa. Thank goodness my bare legs aren't touching the prickly surface of the couch. Mom is wearing one of her cotton house dresses. I look down to her canvas espadrilles and her soft, thin white crew socks.

My attention is drawn back to her arms which cradle me against her while I hold a book in my hands. I focus on her voice. Mom begins reading one of the Little Golden Books: *Good Morning, Good Night.*

Once I was able to read on my own, I chose stories about the paradox of life. When Bambi's mother was shot, I sobbed, but was soon soothed by his friendship with a bunny and a little skunk. I was overjoyed when Bambi reunited with his father, who then taught him how to live in the forest. I was delighted when Bambi met Faline, and when they became parents.

I learned and understood how Bambi could feel two things at one time. He was sad watching his father walk away and, at the same time, filled with joy as he looked at his two new fawns.

Trips to the library would have me scurrying to a special section. I'd plop my little body down in front of all the children's books about the great composers, fascinated by them all. Many of their stories were tragic. Liszt lost his beloved sister, Mozart's relationship with his father was troubled, and Beethoven went deaf but somehow, miraculously, continued to compose.

In early adolescence, I read every series I could find on horses. In each one, the horse faced something appalling. Black Beauty's first owner was kind and generous, but he was sold over and over to a series of owners who mistreated him. Finally, a new owner recognized the beauty that lies somewhere inside the frail, shriveled body, and Black Beauty spent the rest of his days being well treated and put out to pasture.

Through all this reading, I learned that these characters had no choice. An enormous power had been exerted over them. They often suffered while in the controlling hands of soulless, inhumane people. Some characters succumbed to life's circumstances—unable to change, unable to find the strength or courage to move ahead. The lives of these characters often ended badly.

Of course, my favorite characters were the ones that never gave up. They made mistakes, learned from them, and kept trying. They thought a problem through, changed direction, and persevered.

So, I knew that life wasn't always going to be peaches and cream, that I was not guaranteed an easy road. I saw things in my favorite characters that showed me what kind of person I wanted to be: I wanted to be resilient. I wanted to make the choices that developed a positive me. If twists and turns, ups and downs, and mistakes and failures were a part of life, as these stories were telling me, then my favorite life-enhancing characters must have known something that I didn't. Because there was some meaning I was still missing.

I wasn't afraid of my feelings, but none of the books I read told me what to do with them. All I knew was that if I could crawl into the inside of any of those books, the characters there would understand me. They wouldn't make me feel like I was strange, or malformed, or broken. I'd belong in that world just as I was. The books told me my feelings were okay.

Why wasn't I getting those messages at home?

Whenever I'd try to find words to express a feeling—other than joy —Mom would stiffen. "Yvonne, you'd be so much happier if you didn't wear your heart on your sleeve." She was telling me I was too sensitive, but I didn't know how to change that. When my older brother was mean to me and I turned to Mom for help, either I was overreacting, or it was somehow my fault. No one seemed to care. Escaping into my books was all about belonging because I didn't see where else in the real world I fit.

3

Chicks and Chicken Dinner

*O*ur house sat on a small hill. Behind it was a flat grassy spot where Dad parked the car, then another hill, on the crest of which perched Mom's garden.

Mom would sow the seeds, or sometimes just lumps of old potatoes and carrots, and the rain, sun, and earth would unleash what I thought must be magical power because soon new sprouts would push up through the soil and over the summer transform into fresh summer meals and canned goods to see us through the winter.

I'd follow Mom into the garden in the fall, and together we'd pull the dead or dying plants that had served their purpose by producing their life-sustaining roots or fruits, the season's cycle complete.

When I was eight, Mom created a little science experiment for me. She gave me an empty can, told me to fill it with soil from the garden, then showed me how to place a kernel of corn in the soil, just so. At first, Mom reminded me daily to touch the soil to see if it needed water. Seeing nothing happening for many days, I feared the can would only ever hold a bunch of black dirt. Much to my childhood surprise, the kernel soon sprouted and grew. However, when Mom's daily reminders stopped, so did my soil-touching. And soon my little plant wilted and died. And I cried.

Mom had little sympathy for me. "It's a living thing, Yvonne. When you give up, it gives up. If you forget to care for it, it will die."

There were several Easters when a tall-sided box would arrive, tiny brightly colored baby chicks in purple, blue, deep pink, and green inside. My three siblings and I would draw straws to see who would get to pick first, to choose our favorite color. We'd shine a light into the box of chicks to keep them warm and we'd give them food and water. But it wasn't unusual to wake up in the morning and find one of the chicks had died.

After Mom soothed our teary faces, she would help us to prepare an appropriate burial. We'd line a shoe box with something soft, place the baby chick inside, and dig a small grave. We'd say a prayer we learned in church before filling the grave in with dirt.

I was barely a teenager when my responsibilities included slaughtering one of the chickens for dinner. Mom pointed out which chicken she wanted, and I set about the task. I corralled the doomed fowl, placed its neck on the stump by the chicken house, gave it a forceful whack with a hatchet, and severed the head with one strike. It would run around, exactly like a chicken with its head cut off. After it collapsed on the ground, I hung it upside down by its legs on a chicken wire fence where it stayed until it bled out. It wasn't one of my more pleasant chores, but it didn't seem to be overwhelmingly hard. And I only needed to wait until dinner for the reward.

It was around this same time—my early teens—when I first visited a funeral home. The deceased was a friend of the family, someone I'd liked. Dad and Mom told us to be quiet and respectful and to wait patiently in line to greet the family. They'd do the talking, they said. When we reached the casket, we were to kneel and silently say a prayer. After my prayer, mimicking what I'd seen someone ahead of me in the line do, I stood, reached into the casket, and patted the dry cold hand of the corpse.

It all struck me as bizarre: the atmosphere of the funeral home was stiff and formal, seeming as cold and unfeeling as our dead friend's hand. The people in the room seemed not to know what to do or say. Clouds of discomfort stuck to my clothes and got into my hair, an insidious portend of things to come.

Mom's lessons with the kernels of corn, colorful chicks, and our chicken dinners helped me understand that death was a normal part of the living process. I wasn't prepared for how personal it would become, nor how to deal with the emotional impact that ensured that I was ill-prepared to bury loved ones and say goodbye.

WHEN I WAS ABOUT SEVENTEEN, MOM TOLD ME THE STORY OF HOW MY birth was also her near-death experience. She remembered the details vividly.

In 1946, when Mom was pregnant with me and knee deep in labor, Dad brought her to the hospital where she asked for a private room. None was available. Mom, an intensely private woman, was incensed.

Labor and delivery went as planned. After sunset, all was as quiet as only a hospital can be during the night. Mom was asleep, the lights in her shared room turned off. In the middle of the night, Mom's roommate woke to use the bathroom. She heard a sound that shouldn't have been there. From the floor underneath Mom's bed came a *drip, drip, drip*. Mom was hemorrhaging.

Mom told me she recalled going through a crystal-white tunnel, filled with a sublime peace she'd never felt before. She knew in her soul that Dad, my older brother Mickey, and I—her newborn—would be perfectly fine. Wherever she was and wherever she was going, she was more content than she had ever been.

She described floating above herself and the hospital bed and watching as the nurses and a doctor rushed in, concern on their faces, and furiously began lifesaving measures. After some time, she heard their sighs of relief. "That was close, but she's going to be okay," she heard the doctor say.

Mom was *not* relieved. She viewed the scene below, first in disbelief and then horror. Finally, filled with anger, she realized she was coming back. How dare they pluck her from that place of absolute serenity?

Mom told me that this experience made her unafraid of dying. She knew what was waiting on the other side and it was wonderful.

Mothers pass things onto their daughters.

Mess Up the Fishing

*D*ad loved to fish. My two uncles and my older brother were Dad's fishing buddies, and the three of them would often take off for a morning or an afternoon of fishing. I wasn't invited.

I was pretty good at cleaning fish. Dad had rested an old door flat on top of two sawhorses, which I'd cover with newspaper. I preferred it if the fish were already dead, but to impress Dad I'd whack them on the head if I had to. I'd cut off the head, slit the belly, gut and scoop out the innards, and remove all of the scales. Crappies were my favorite. Their scales slipped right off as I slid the knife from the tail to the head. Or where the head had been. Then I'd plop the cleaned fish into a bucket of clean water underneath the table, wrap all the heads and gooey entrails in newspaper, and deposit the mess in a garbage pail. I'd take the bucket of cleaned fish into the kitchen, drain it, and rinse each fish by hand under the spigot. I'd finished the job only when the fish were either cooking on the stove or packaged and placed in the freezer.

I was also pretty good at finding the night crawlers Dad and the boys used for bait. The best time was after a rain when the big, juicy worms would come up to the surface and lay atop the wet grass. Off we'd go, Dad holding the flashlight. The trick was to shine the light on the grass to see a worm peeking out of a hole but move the light quickly away so the night crawler wouldn't shrink back into its hole so I could quickly snatch it. Squeeze or pull too hard and the earthworm would break. We wanted whole, live night crawlers. We'd keep them in a large dirt-filled coffee tin in the refrigerator, waiting for the next fishing trip.

But I was never invited to go fishing. One day as the guys were planning the next day's fishing trip, feeling pretty brave, I said, "Dad, I want to go along."

"No, this is just for the guys."

But Mom chimed in, her voice harder than usual. "Oh Mike, take her. It's not going to hurt anything." To my surprise and delight, Dad agreed.

One of Dad's favorite fishing places was along French Creek near Meadville, Pennsylvania, at Wilson's Chute. We walked along the hard-packed, rust-brown dirt trail by the side of the stream. The path was so narrow we had to walk in a single file, hemmed in on both sides with willowy vegetation that towered well over my head. The metal bucket I swung at my side brushed the bushes. To the left the land swept gently uphill, dense with oak and beech trees. To the right, I could hear the gentle rushing of the creek.

Dad parked me at an opening in the vegetation and gave me a pole. He attached the red-and-white round bobber to the line, at the perfect distance from the weighted hook so the bait hung at the right depth in the stream.

I already knew how to thread a slimy night crawler onto the hook without flinching, weaving them in and out of the hook and leaving a small piece free on the end. Dad showed me how to cast, and how to press the button to release the clear fishing line.

"Don't pull back on the pole right away when the bobber goes under. Wait until it's really under then give the pole a little tug. But don't pull too hard or you'll lose the fish."

It was a beautiful sunny day, I was fishing with Dad, and I was happy. I heard the plopping sound of the bobber hitting the water and watched as it started to drift downstream with the current.

"You stay here, I don't want you to come to where we are 'cause you'll just mess up the fishing." And with that, he walked downstream to the guys. I could no longer see him. I was very much on my own.

I was too content to be out fishing "with the boys" to realize what he'd done, my ten-year-old self blissfully unaware that this might be a ripple cascading through my relationship with Dad.

And then it happened. The bobber began to bounce in the water. I knew something was nibbling and I waited, my heart racing. When the bobber went under the second time, I gave the pole a little tug. I felt it catch, and I knew I had something. I was careful to reel the line in slowly, give it some slack, then reel some more until I pulled my catch onto the bank.

"Dad!"

Silence.

"DAD!"

"What do you want?" The impatience clear in his voice.

"I caught a fish."

He came back along the trail with a stringer in hand, a light metal chain that had lock snaps along its length. The snap would open, like a safety pin, and a metal wire was thread up through the fish's gill and out the mouth. Dad showed me how to use it, and he put the stringer with the fish attached back into the stream so we could keep it alive and fresh. Dad anchored the stringer into the bank beside me and set back off to his own spot by the creek.

I called him twice more that day, and the guys didn't catch any. I was proud of myself. I had outdone them. And in particular, I had bested my dad. *Don't say I'll mess up the fishing. I'll show you*, I thought, the seeds of opposition taking root.

The Great Divide

*D*ad would sometimes talk about a job he had in the south in the early 1940s, before the war. He'd tell us about the boarding house he lived in, referring to the servants as "darkies." I understand that he was using the common vernacular of the time, but it revealed an attitude about African Americans that made me uncomfortable. As I grew into adulthood, we argued about race relations. A lot.

And then I accepted a teaching position in an all-Black school in Cleveland, Ohio. He was not happy.

"What the hell did you go and do that for?" he spat.

"Because I want to make a difference," I reasoned.

"You can make a difference right here in your hometown."

I was tired of this now-familiar prelude to a race argument. "I am going to do it in Cleveland," I retorted, a little more hotly than necessary.

That's how many of our conversations would go. It was like we were on a tennis court. Lob and return, lob and return. We'd deliver our words with a *whack,* and the other would smash them back with a harder, faster retort. Neither of us would back down. Neither of us would let the other win. The match would end with one of us turning forcefully and walking away.

One Thanksgiving, we had traveled to another state to spend the holiday with Dad's niece. Dad did all of the driving, Mother was in the front seat beside him, and Aunt Josephine and I sat in the back. We managed the four-hour drive together without a cross word about some social issue. In fact, there wasn't much conversation at all, which suited me just fine.

The women were in the kitchen preparing food, and the men, my niece's boys included, were in the TV room watching football. There was lots of laughter coming from both rooms. All the burners and the oven were on, condensation coating the kitchen windows like gray clouds before a rain. The house was filled with wonderful aromas of the deliciousness to come.

Nine of us gathered around the table, prepared to sit for several hours. The courses flowed according to Italian tradition. First there was Italian wedding soup, followed by an antipasto. Next, pasta with sauce and Italian sausage. Finally, turkey, stuffing, sweet potato casserole, and green beans would be served. Pumpkin and apple pie along with ricotta cheese pie would finish the meal.

I never made it to the turkey course. Somehow, when I wasn't looking, the conversation slipped to the subject of race.

There were plenty of hot-button race issues during that time, and Dad and I saw opposite sides of every one of them. Segregation, Martin Luther King Jr., my teaching job in Cleveland. He swung a strong overhand serve, and I returned with a forceful backhand. Back and forth, back and forth. In good Italian fashion, the conversation got more heated and louder with each passing moment. The rest of the table fell silent.

Aunt Josephine spoke up and chastised me. "Don't you talk to your papa like that!"

That just added fuel to my fire, an explosion against his resistance to my reasoning imminent. Then my brain kicked in with a warning:

Don't say another word, Yvonne. Because if you do, it will be something you'll never be able to take back. Where that wisdom came from, I'm not sure, but I'm grateful that it did.

I pushed my chair back from the table. "I'm going for a walk."

"Good idea," Dad said, his face red.

"You apologize to your papa first," said Aunt Josephine.

I threw a fiery look in her direction, grabbed my coat, and stormed out the kitchen door. I didn't know the neighborhood, so I kept walking around the same large block. I reached the end of one street, turned right, turned right again and again until I passed the house. I was locked in my own head and didn't notice anyone or anything else. Over and over, I played with all the things I could have said, should have said, wished I'd said. How could he—in this day and age—continue to believe those things? How could he, who had suffered at the end of the prejudicial stick for being Italian, continue to say what he said?

The sky had begun to darken when I finally headed back inside. The walk had helped my anger subside, but it was replaced with a deep, aching sadness. How could I be this man's daughter? He was a blowhard, talking up a good racist line in white company, then being perfectly decent and respectful when any Black person—or other ethnic minority—was standing in front of him looking him in the eye. Was he being insincere? Or, as I suspected was the case, was he a walking contradiction?

I must have been gone for hours. By the time I arrived back at the house, the table had been cleared, and the dishes were done. The dining room was dark. Mom was sitting on the couch, but she looked up when I came into the room.

"I've been waiting for you. Your father has gone to bed, as have the others."

"I had to leave before I said something really hurtful."

Her face was sober, her eyes clear but sad. "Yvonne, if you want to know your father, you will have to go to him. He isn't going to change.

If you are ever to have the relationship you want with him, you'll have to make that happen."

I took her words to heart and little by little I shifted how I responded to Dad. I tried to meet him where he was.

I avoided anything that might trigger an argument. I talked about things I knew would interest him. I asked his advice. Slowly, the tension between us eased. We weren't yet where I wanted us to be, but we were closer than we'd been.

Several years later, when it was very clear that my dying car could no longer take care of me, Dad suggested it was time I buy a new one.

"Your cousin Tony owns a dealership. Why don't you call him and see what he might have? I think you'd get a really good deal."

It was good advice. Tony gave me a sweet deal on a 1972 Dodge Dart with a slant-six engine. It was a deep forest green with a black vinyl roof. It wasn't my style, but I wasn't prepared to say no to either man. Besides, Tony kept reassuring both Dad and me that the car was safe and reliable.

It was true. What the car lacked in sportiness or elegance it made up for in dependability. It took me back and forth to work, and it was good in the snow. So good that my friends and I always took my car when we went cross-country skiing.

One summer, I called Dad. "I want to come home this weekend. I'm learning to work on the Dart. Is it OK if I grab your toolbox?"

"You're learning to work on your car?" His voice was tinged with disbelief.

"Yup. The spark plugs and oil need to be changed."

That Saturday, a sparkling June day with clear blue skies and a gentle breeze, I raised the garage door and backed the car halfway in. I grabbed Dad's toolbox and went to work.

I was loosening one of the spark plugs when Dad came out and leaned on the front left fender, peering under the hood to see if I knew what I was doing.

"You know, it always bothered me that you went to your mother for advice and you didn't come to me," Dad said. "I know it's because you don't want to hear what I have to say."

I pulled out the first spark plug, turned to face him, and looked him in the eye.

"No Dad, it wasn't that. It was that you didn't *talk* to me. You were always yelling."

I had come to where he was that day. He and I had crossed a great divide. And the gruff tone that had made me afraid disappeared—mostly—into the rear-view mirror.

6

The Magnificent Mark

*I*n 1978, my youngest brother Mark—twenty-six years old—
invited the thirty-one-year-old me to join him in Pittsburgh
for a weekend. We'd be staying with his girlfriend who was also my
best friend, Mary Catherine. Mark brought a friend along, providing
me with a date. We planned to go to Wheeling, West Virginia for a
Gordon Lightfoot concert.

The concert was spectacular. The next day, we spent several hours
walking around one of the largest music stores in the country. I
meandered through the aisles, circling back periodically to find Mark.
He'd pick up a guitar and strum a little, then move on and try another.
He spent what felt like a ridiculous amount of time sifting through
record collections and seemed to be in his element. He finally came
looking for me saying it was time to leave, he'd found what he wanted:
a wafer-thin, brown onion-skin paper bag was tucked under his arm.

When we got to the car, he pulled a piece of sheet music from the
bag and beamed as he shared his prize. It was the music and lyrics of
"Dust in the Wind," the song made popular by the band Kansas. I was
incredulous. All that time for that piece of music? What had he been

thinking? I told him I thought the music was glorious, but the lyrics were hauntingly dismal.

"The words simply tell the truth," Mark said. "Everything we do passes into insignificance. When it's over, money won't matter. We aren't going to be here forever, we're simply specks on a timeline."

I was grateful when the depressing conversation ended. It seemed to me that we were four young people sitting in Mark's Peugeot—three people with a ton of time ahead of us. We weren't insignificant. Life did matter. An uneasy silence filled the car, each of us locked into our own thoughts.

Sometimes, with Mark, I felt I wasn't deep enough, that I just couldn't keep up with his thoughts. Then I'd feel a little upset: why did he always have to be so intense? Why did he gravitate to subjects that were polarizing? Why couldn't we just talk about nice things?

That weekend was no different: why did he have to be so enamored with a song that talked about death? Why couldn't this be the light-hearted, fun weekend that I needed? Here we were, together for the first time in months. We lived forty miles apart and were both busy. I had been looking forward to music and laughter.

Mary Catherine broke the spell and suggested pizza and beer for lunch. "Just wait until you taste the pizza. I promise," she said as we slid into a booth that had seen better days—brown vinyl with holes patched by bright orange duct tape. Thank goodness for the sun pouring through the bay window at the front of the restaurant. She was right about the food.

The conversation shifted to the kind I'd wanted. We were the only ones in the restaurant, and we were soon laughing so hard the sound was ricocheting off the wood walls. The servers seemed to enjoy the fun as much as we did; the pizza and beer indeed made up for the shortcomings in the décor.

When I arrived home Sunday evening, I called Mark and told him how special the weekend had been. We each shared what spending time together had meant and, as we neared the end of the call, he said,

"It was so good to be with you, and I want you to know how much I love you."

"I love you too," I said. "Let's not have so much time in between this visit and the next. I love you, bro."

Three days later, in the early hours of the morning, I was shocked out of sleep by an ominous ringing. It was Dad on the phone.

Mark's little Peugeot had hit a bridge abutment while driving to see Mary Catherine. The coroner told Dad Mark had died instantly.

I immediately began to regret how I'd handled the conversation around "Dust in the Wind." What else made the song resonate so with him? How did he feel about death and dying? What did he think happened to someone after they passed? What was his spiritual anchor?

Because of my discomfort and resistance to the subject matter, all of those questions would forever remain unanswered, the opportunity to become closer with my brother forever lost.

7

Learning To Ski

*J*n my late twenties, I received an invitation from a close friend to come to Vermont and visit over the Christmas vacation.

She rented a house that sat at the top of a hill and shared it with a drop-dead-gorgeous male roommate. What's-his-name was well over six feet tall, his abundance of wavy dark brown hair with hints of gold setting off a porcelain-smooth complexion, finely chiseled features, and soft blue eyes. Besides being wonderful to look at, he held a PhD and taught at a local university. Smarts and good looks—what a package.

They lived in a large and welcoming log cabin. The wood stove in the living room generated warmth that didn't quite make it to my room. Every room had windows that looked out over snow-covered hills and valleys. There were no other homes in view, which sometimes made me feel isolated. Overcast and snowy outside, the wood-log walls created a sense of calm and peace. Blue, sunny days were breathtaking. The temperatures were such that the sun made the snow sparkle everywhere my head turned.

After dinner on my very first evening, my friend handed me her cross-country ski boots. "If you're going to be in Vermont in the winter, you're going to have to learn to ski," she said. I wasn't at all sure it was something I'd be able to do. I'd never participated in sports. I loathed doing anything in front of people that would show my lack of coordination or my ineptitude.

My face must have betrayed me because she immediately turned reassuring. "It's really easy once you get the hang of it." She explained that her roommate had agreed to teach me. Her handsome roommate. I felt a case of lockjaw coming on.

My head rattled with "You've got to be kidding." This repeated—over and over—as I stood there stock-still and filled with trepidation. I was literally going out in the snow on this star-sparkled evening to be taught to ski by a gorgeous college biology professor.

I followed him out of the house like a puppy after its master. My teacher put his own skis on first and looped his hands up and through the straps on his poles, then showed me how to do the same. We stood beside each other in the flat field. He took several strides, then stopped, instructing me to approach him without using my poles. He said it would allow me to develop better balance and stability, explaining that I should avoid the temptation to push the skis with my toes.

When I reached him, he gently took hold of my elbow and encouraged me to ski beside him, still without poles. When I was comfortable doing that, he showed me how to use the poles: the leg that was pushing had the pole planted in the snow behind the heel of the boot, while the opposite arm lifted and stretched out in front.

Of course, I landed on my keester several times, and he showed me how to get up. By the end of the lesson, I was gliding clumsily across the snow. But I could see that the movement on the skis was so natural. I returned to the cabin with a Cheshire grin on my face. I had done it. I'd swallowed my embarrassment and clumsiness. And I loved it. Being out on the snow, body warm from the inside out, achieving the movement and rhythm and basking in the beauty of the night under the moonlight and twinkling stars.

When I returned home, I purchased all my own gear. I encouraged friends to come with me to a ski lodge not far from town. Not only was I hooked, but my friends became enthusiastic partners.

8

The Calling

My life wasn't working the way I wanted it to. I was happy enough, and I had a successful teaching career. I loved my job, and I loved the students I taught. They gave my life meaning and purpose. I had really good friends and an active social life.

What I didn't have was a fulfilling and lasting relationship with a man. I would date, but each relationship would end in some miserable way. Either I would decide he wasn't the one for me, or the guy would announce it just wasn't working.

As year after year passed, my dream of being married and having a family began to slip away. I was in my early thirties. The old body clock was ticking and the ability to carry a child safely to term seemed more remote.

When I reflected on my life, it had been focused on school: I started school in 1951 and graduated in 1964. I went on to Edinboro University of Pennsylvania until 1969. After that, as an undergrad in elementary education, I taught in Cleveland for a semester. I taught in my hometown, Meadville, as well, which meant I could live at home with my parents. Over the next ten years I worked in the Human Relations

Commission as the only Caucasian on staff, leaving that position to go back to teaching. I went on to obtain my master's degree in elementary education and the certification necessary to become an elementary school principal.

But something was missing.

I had tried therapy years before and, after three sessions, I thought I didn't need to go anymore. I told myself that I had this thing in the bag. I couldn't have said then or now *what* was in the bag, but I was sure *it* was in there. The big block lettering on the outside of my proverbial bag said DENIAL.

Another dismal breakup prompted me to try therapy again. My hand shook as I picked up the phone and called a psychologist that had been recommended to me. His voice was soft and reassuring, and he asked some questions to get a sense of what I was looking for.

My heart thumped like a heavy metal band's bass drum all the way to his office. My complexion must have been white as I approached the receptionist to give her my name. I sat on the edge of the couch closest to the door in case I wanted to bolt. When the therapist opened the door and called my name, my legs and feet were unsteady as I stood and walked through the office door. Once inside, the room seemed to close in. I just knew there was about to be a showdown with my mother's advice not to wear my heart on my sleeve.

His questions were general, the kind I would have asked if I were meeting someone new. He was relaxed, almost friendly, and disarming. As the minutes passed, my shoulders dropped, and I slid back into the comfort of the couch. A refreshing ease set in. The fifty-minute session was over before I knew it. I booked my next appointment for the following week.

This therapy was different to the other time. This therapist made me feel like he cared about me. At the same time, he gently pushed me when I needed to open my eyes a little to see something from a new perspective.

I was more than a little surprised when he started talking about my being depressed. I knew that there was a history of depression in my family—my uncle and cousin had committed suicide, after all—but I thought I'd escaped it. I certainly didn't behave in the ways that I had seen in other family members who were depressed. I wasn't reclusive, nor did I have difficulty holding a job. I was active, successful, and productive, but I began to see how a cloud of underlying sorrow impacted me and the choices that I made.

When the psychologist suggested medication, I resisted. Was there anything else I could do besides popping some kind of pill? He suggested exercise, particularly aerobic. I bought Jane Fonda cassette and VHS exercise tapes and moved my body until I broke out in a sweat. I loved the music and dance routines and miraculously, I got my therapist's recommended hour of aerobic exercise six days a week.

The fog indeed began to lift a little, and the therapist started having me look at my coping mechanisms and diving into feelings. I learned that my feelings weren't the problem. They were signals that something was off. He wanted me to drill down and find out what was causing them in the first place.

Which led us to a series of sessions where we focused on my relationship with Dad. The more I shared, and my therapist guided, I began to shift my perspective on my father. Instead of wishing he was different, more open, that he would demonstrate his feelings for me, I began to come to terms with the fact that Dad was who he was. I began to see that it was holding onto these emotionally immature wishes about my father that was holding me back—my father wasn't doing that. When I could let go of my expectations for Dad and love him for who he was, I'd be happier. And my therapist made it clear that until I did this work, I would never find a partner for the loving marriage relationship I so desired.

I'll never forget the pivotal session. "Yvonne, when are you going to stop being the breast to the world?" I jolted upright—I'm glad he couldn't read my mind, although the expression on my face would have given him a clue. My expression had turned to stone. The *breast to the world?* Seriously?

I wanted to bound up off the sofa and deck him. How dare he ask me such a crass question? I was livid but said nothing. My tone was flat as I answered other questions, and we talked a little more. When I left his office, I wrenched the car door open, plopped my butt into the driver's seat, and drove through town with both hands clenched tight on the steering wheel. Every car in front of me, every building that I passed, and every stoplight that impeded my progress fed into my growing, overwhelming anger. How dare he?

Breast to the world? The words ricocheted all week long. I wasn't trying to save anyone. I was attempting to be the best, most compassionate teacher and friend I could be. I was working on letting those close to me know how much I cared. All I wanted to do was to be helpful. Breast to the world indeed. I was ready to spit those words right back at him at our next session.

As the days passed, I began to understand that I had come far enough in therapy that I was ready for the question, no matter how much it stung. It was a question that I needed to address. My life and career had centered around the proposition that I never wanted anyone to hurt as badly as I sometimes had. So yes, I suppose I was out to save the world. It was an admirable goal, but it cost me.

It kept me from setting clear boundaries and had me reaching too far. I kept trying to help in situations that I wasn't trained for. I kept digging in and becoming too involved, with the result that I became totally ineffective. It kept me from seeing the danger signs that were right in front of my face. I didn't see that a student was far too troubled and beyond the scope of my expertise.

It kept me thinking each guy I was dating would surely change if I just kept loving him with my whole being. My father would surely change if I just kept showing him how much I could achieve, which was a twisted attempt to gain his praise. I was that little kid fascinated by the heat coming from the top of the stove. I kept reaching for the warmth. How many times had I stretched my hand too close, only to get burned?

I didn't want to lose what drove me to be a good daughter, sibling, friend, and teacher. If trying to be a savior was the source of much of my angst, what would be the replacement? What could I do that would be helpful to myself and those that I cared about? I wanted to be helpful, but how could I do that without harming myself? And I was harming myself.

I loved reading self-help books. They posed the realism of living life. They threw out that not all stories had fairy tale endings. They exposed me to the idea that life is difficult and then, sometimes, it is extremely difficult.

The theories in those books—the why things were difficult—were comforting. I was learning why things were the way they were, but there was something in each book that was lacking. I wanted a how-to manual. Okay, so sometimes I was going to get hurt or frustrated or angry. It wasn't pleasant but, as they say, it is what it is. What I wanted to learn, step by step, even if painful, was how to cope.

I wanted to learn coping skills, and not only for myself. If I learned how to cope, I could teach those same skills to others.

Therapy took a turn. I became more adept at seeing warning signals and putting on the brakes. I became more sensitive to what I was experiencing and found ways of dealing with situations more effectively. I could see the end of the road, and I felt that I was coming to the end of my need for therapy.

In one of our last sessions, something came out of my mouth unbidden. My face lit up like a Christmas tree as a new awareness came rushing in. My smile deepened as I said firmly, "You know, I think I could do this work. I think I want to be a psychotherapist."

"Yes, you very much could do this work," my therapist said in return. Tears of relief and joy filled my eyes.

Graduate school could be an extension to developing a more comprehensive how-to manual. The word that was most important was how. I could learn a boatload of skills that would help people, including myself. I was ready for a new adventure, and I was eager to hit the road.

And so it was: while I taught—my second decade of teaching—I returned to school to obtain my master's in clinical psychology. I would resign after twenty years of teaching and begin my work as a psychotherapist.

9

Meeting Kirk

I called my then boyfriend to have the phone answered by a female voice. "Who is this?" I asked. "I'm his girlfriend," she said. It took awhile to grieve and cry as I said goodbye to yet another relationship dream. But a message started coming slowly through the mist that was lifting. The message was in my voice, a little halting at first, but day after day becoming more insistent. "The signs have been there from the beginning and I chose to ignore them. Never again, I'm done."

For the next four years, I rarely dated, and when I did, if the same old signs were there, I was upfront and stubborn. Not interested.

I was helping a good friend, Shannon, pack up and move out of her apartment and out of the city. We lived in the same complex, a refurbished building on the national historic registry. I walked down the hall, and her door was ajar. When I stepped in, I wasn't greeted by her, but there stood a tall male beauty with the blonde good looks of Robert Redford. Our eyes locked and it was immediate and electric. We were introduced, and throughout the day of packing Shannon's stuff, we were both keenly aware of the physical attraction, and I wasn't surprised when he asked for my phone number.

His call came shortly thereafter, and my breath caught and a red flag appeared with his specific date request. "Why don't you come over to my house and cook dinner?"

My response was quick and sure. "How about we meet at a restaurant and how about we make it Dutch?

"Great idea."

The restaurant I suggested was within walking distance of my apartment. I entered and saw him waving to me from a table in the middle of the restaurant. After the simple greetings that polite behavior required and ordering drinks, we began to talk. Or should I say, he began to talk.

I learned about his wonderful job and how well he was doing with his company. He shared how it afforded him the sleek, high-powered car he drove and his beautiful house. He described each room in colorful detail. I smiled, nodded, and I listened. Never once did he ask about me or what I did. He didn't ask me anything and the red flags kept bouncing all around me.

When dinner was over the street lamps were on, I appreciated his offer to walk me back to my apartment. When we stepped inside the foyer, he took my hand and leaned in to deliver a kiss on the cheek.

"I'll give you a call," he said.

"Thank you, but I don't think you will. In fact, I would rather that you didn't."

Unlocking the door and stepping into my apartment, everything looked somewhat different. It wasn't as if the furniture had been changed or even rearranged. The artwork, the baskets hanging on the walls, and all of the lush green plants, were in the exactly the same spots. It was as welcoming as it had always been. What had changed?

And then it hit me. My apartment hadn't changed. I had. The change was profound.

I had just turned a mammoth corner, and the view around it was life altering. I was happy and comfortable in my own skin. I enjoyed being single and all that it meant. As much as I had wanted children of my own, I realized I loved having classrooms full of them. I loved being with friends, but the time I spent alone was satisfying in a way it had never been before. I might feel lonely at times, but I never felt alone.

I started researching for things that I would like to do. I signed up for Irish stepdance classes. When I found an Irish music festival two hour's drive away, I went. I saw a table of folks with a sign that said they were from Erie, and I asked if I could join them.

I did things that brought me pleasure. I was hooked on the movie *Amadeus*, and I went to see it eight times. Each time, I chose to go by myself.

When the loneliness appeared, I found ways to be with friends. When a birthday with one of those wonderful zeros was approaching, I planned my own party at a local restaurant, and I invited folks to join me.

About two weeks before Thanksgiving, Shannon called and said she was coming into the city. What did I think about having a girls' Thanksgiving dinner together?

We all pitched in and the table was laden with all the trimmings: turkey, stuffing, mashed potatoes, home-made bread, and pumpkin pie. We laughed and talked through all of the courses, and as we sat eating pie with whipped cream and sipping the accompanying cups of coffee, Shannon turned to me. "Yvonne, I met this really neat guy and I think the two of you should talk."

"Yeah, right." I laughed. "That's all I need."

When Shannon gets an idea, she generally pushes through. "No, I think you were meant for each other. I'll give him a call and tell him all about you. And I'll give you his number. Actually, where is your address book? I'll put it in there right now."

The number could be in my address book, but that didn't mean I had to do anything with it. Except that I did.

It was February, and I was happily spending another Saturday night alone watching TV. I picked up the phone and called this stranger whose name was Kirk.

"Hello," said the warm voice after the first ring.

"Hi, Kirk? It's Yvonne."

There was the barest pause. "Oh, of course. You're Shannon's friend, right?"

For the next hour and a half, we talked. It was easy and fluid. He asked questions, and I answered. I asked questions, and he answered. We each seemed interested in what the other had to say.

The conversation came to a close when Kirk's six-year-old daughter Kate started crawling on the top of the couch behind him. It was his weekend to have his children. Kate and her brother Peter had been watching a movie in the family room. Now she was bored with it and wanted to play.

"Yvonne, I need to get my kids into bed. Thank you for calling, and I'll call you soon." A few days later, Kirk left a message on my answering machine, saying he'd call again later. Which he didn't. As much as I'd enjoyed that first conversation, I was non-plussed that I didn't hear from him again.

The months passed and I forgot all about Kirk—until Shannon called and reminded me. She insisted that I get in contact again.

"He's not dating anyone else, there is no other woman, but he has had some family issues to deal with. You're going to Hershey to speak at the state conference. That's not far from where he lives. Just pick up the phone and see what happens."

So, I called. Kirk said he'd take me out to dinner, but I had to choose the restaurant. Keeping my own safety in mind, I asked him to meet me in the lobby at the Hershey Lodge.

At the appointed time, I began to descend the circular staircase leading to the lobby from the second floor. It reminded me of a scene from an old Humphrey Boggart movie. I was wearing a blush pink suit with a cream-colored silk blouse and a string of pearls at my neck.

Kirk was standing at the bottom of the staircase, looking up. He wore a gray wool business suit with soft blue lines running through it. Over his arm was a trench coat and in his left hand was a felt fedora. Kirk looked nothing like anyone I had ever gone out with before.

In the car all the way to the restaurant, we talked. He was obviously nervous because he cut a turn too close, bouncing off the triangular cement traffic island. Seeming to need something to cut through his anxiousness, he put a cassette tape in the stereo, announcing, "This is one of the most beautiful pieces of music I have ever heard. It's the 'Faure Requiem.' I hope you like choral work."

I didn't say it, but it's not every day that a girl gets a requiem played for her on a first date. Secretly, I thought the evening was looking up.

When we sat at our table, the talking started again. The poor waitress kept approaching to ask if we were ready to order. Finally, on her fourth try, we gave in and ordered.

When dinner was finished and Kirk had driven me back to my hotel, Kirk asked if I'd like to go for a walk before he had to get back home. I agreed, with a request that I go back to my room and change into a pair of jeans and some sneakers.

When I got back home, Shannon called. "So how did it go?"

My answer was quick and precise. "I think this guy has possibilities."

Those possibilities have sustained a marriage that has lasted more than thirty years.

10

Learning to Listen

$\mathcal{H}$e wasn't a handsome man, but the wire frame glasses on his face were like a window into his gentle character. His thin hair was peppered gray; he was of medium height and of slight build. Although he was soft-spoken, his words traveled purposely through the air, laden with meaning. He was the professor in one of the required courses, in 1983, to complete my master's degree in clinical psychology.

It was an evening class, which meant I'd come directly from work. I had just enough time to grab a sandwich before the two-hour lecture. Even with the overhead lights, the classroom was dark, and the seating was less than comfortable. I had to work hard to stay awake and focus.

One evening, the gentle professor delivered a simple sentence in a stronger voice than usual, as if it was a reprimand.

"The hardest thing you will have to do as a psychologist is to listen."

The hardest thing? My inner voice scoffed at his statement. Listening was going to be a piece of cake in a session. All I had to do was to sit there and keep my mouth shut, keep looking at the person seated across from me, watch their expression and posture, and pay attention to their word choice. Hard indeed.

It wasn't until the following year, 1984, when I had my first adult client during my internship at a pediatric and adolescent mental health unit in a local hospital. It was the last thing I had to do before being granted my master's degree. It was there that I began to understand the professor's message and experience for myself just how hard listening was.

My first client was a young woman in her thirties with anxiety and depression that were negatively impacting her functioning and relationships. I was nervous. No, I was scared to death. How was I going to facilitate for fifty minutes? How was I supposed to start? What questions would I ask?

After greeting each other, I said, "What brings you into therapy? What would you like to accomplish?"

My professor's words kept ringing in my ears. Listening *was* hard work. I had to focus on what my client was saying to me in a totally different way than during regular conversations with colleagues and friends. If my mind drifted, I had to pull myself back. I had to pay attention to every word, to the tone of voice, tilt of head, and connect with the emotions just below the surface. I had to set aside my own nervousness and all my own whirling thoughts while I was with that client.

She revealed that when her husband came home a few days before, she was angry with him. She'd had a gun in her lap and was prepared to use it on him. Which, thankfully, she didn't do. That brought my focus immediately to the room and to her. I realized that this was a detail I was not going to be able to keep in confidence, and I told her that.

When the session came to a close and the client agreed to return for another session, I was relieved. I wasn't quite ready to pat myself on the back for a job well done, but I believed the session went okay. And given what she shared with me I knew there was more work to do.

My supervisor was waiting for me in his office for a debrief.

"How'd it go?" he asked me as I sat down heavily.

"I'm exhausted." I was more than a little surprised. This was supposed to be an easy client, my first client, but it felt anything but. I told my supervisor about the gun and that she said she'd been close to using it on her husband. He, in turn, took it up to his boss, and collectively we determined that I would need to call the husband to alert him so he could take necessary steps to protect himself. Which I did.

This was one client, and the session lasted less than an hour. But the enormity of what I heard, and the enormity of discharging my responsibility under the ethics code so huge... how would I manage with a full caseload?

The more clients I saw, the less heavy the task as I built my listening skills. To focus so keenly on their story, I learned not to think of them as bad people doing harmful things, but as wounded, sometimes desperate people who needed help. I made sure they knew they were the most important person in the room. Of course, I was the one asking questions and steering our direction, but it was their storytelling that helped them to examine parts of their life, connect with their narrative, to identify where they wanted to see change, and ultimately to see themselves in a different way. And I began to see how my being with them—and truly listening—was an essential part of the healing process.

As I became more comfortable and proficient, I learned how to hear my clients' stories from a variety of perspectives and to ask open-ended questions which allowed them to find out more about who they were and why they behaved the way that they did. They were able to draw conclusions and come up with ways they could help themselves. They began to create the changes that helped them meet their needs in more appropriate ways.

Many years later, I was working in the employee assistance office of a local mental health institution. Businesses would purchase contracts which would allow their employees to access free, brief counseling sessions. The management at the institution was approached by a therapist who was writing a manual for short-term couples counseling. He wanted to get feedback and refine his work, and to do so he wanted to take a few of us therapists through structured activities he'd created. These were based on a noted marital therapist's work. The exercises would require that we be vulnerable and talk openly about our own marriages. We were to be his guinea pigs.

We met in our director's wood-paneled office, which was large enough to allow us to be seated in an oval. The sofa and plush chairs offered comfort. Sunlight pouring through the big window on the back wall warmed the office. We discussed confidentiality and agreed that what was said would stay in the room.

The instruction for our first activity was to listen to the therapist's question but answer it only in our heads and, when he gave the signal, we were supposed to all say out loud what we were thinking. He repeated the first question several times and asked for silence.

"When interviewing couples for the first time what is the one thing they say is the most problematic in their relationship?"

With a broad grin on his face, he said, "Now, all together, what is your answer?"

Almost in unison, not quite using identical combinations of words but clearly on the same theme, we all answered, "We don't communicate."

The next question, preceded by the same instruction to stay silent until he prompted us to give the answer, was, "What about your partner speaks to the lack of communication?"

To a person we responded either, "He doesn't listen," or, "She doesn't listen." The room erupted in laughter, so loud and boisterous that he reminded us that someone might be out in the waiting room.

We gathered again the following week, eager to see how he'd suggest getting around the difficulties that lack of communication and poor listening caused in a relationship. He explained that he gives his stressed couples-clients an introduction to how the brain works: when we are triggered, our normal response options are fight, flight, freeze, or play dead. These responses are meant for our survival, when we are in danger, but they don't support deep communication. In order to communicate effectively, each person has to create within themselves a feeling of safety.

He led us through an exercise of closing our eyes and visualizing that safe space. He explained that in the next exercise it would be critical for the listener to be in that safe space. He then taught a listening technique called mirroring, also known as active listening. The person who chooses to be the listener has the hardest job. Once finding their safe space, the listener asks their partner to talk about something in the marriage that is distressing. Then, the listener must resist the normal temptation to counter what the partner is saying, and instead to paraphrase what the partner said.

We watched a video demonstrating a therapist guiding a real couple through the mirroring technique. The therapist and the couple were up on a stage. The therapist was in a chair facing the couple, who were seated on a couch. The therapist asked the woman to talk about something in her relationship with her husband that bothered her.

The woman started by saying that it made her extremely anxious if her husband didn't call before he was going to be late. The husband took a minute, and said, "If I heard you correctly," and he paraphrased what she said. She agreed he'd heard what she said.

"Tell me more," the husband then prompted.

The conversation continued in this manner for several minutes, the husband paraphrasing—mirroring—the wife's responses, digging deeper into the roots of this issue. Soon the woman's eyes filled with tears as she talked.

"If I heard you correctly, what happened in your childhood with your alcoholic parents was awful. You never knew what kind of condition they would be in when you came home, or if they were going to safely come home at all," the husband said. "Did I understand you correctly?"

She nodded yes. Her husband sat up straighter on the couch and reached for her hand. He was no longer using the technique, when he said, "Now I understand why it's so important for me to call you when I'm going to be late."

We were witnessing healing as it was taking place in this marriage.

I adopted the mirroring technique in my own practice. My professor was right. To really listen, all of my attention needs to be focused on the other person. Listening was not about me. It was all about them. That takes all my energy. And it is hard work.

11

Mirroring and Meaning

I'd always wanted to spend a chunk of time in Colorado during the winter, and a dear friend agreed to have me come spend a month with her at her home in Colorado Springs. She had to work, so during the weekdays I'd be on my own.

She connected me with friends that would help me satisfy my dream of cross-country skiing in the Rockies.

It was on one of those Colorado-Rocky-Mountain-high days, that my guide—my friend's friend—shared his philosophy with me. Solidly built and a few inches taller than me—I'm an inch over five feet if I pull myself up straight—his cherub-face and ruddy complexion matching his bright red hair, and he immediately made me feel comfortable as we drove to a place where he loved to ski.

The powder beneath our skinny skis was sparkling in the morning sunshine. He led the way, which meant that he had the heavier job of cutting the trail. We circled through a valley of pine trees laden with snow, and at every turn the magic of majestic mountains surrounding us washed over me.

After an hour of pushing through the snow, we stopped near a sizable rock that would act as our picnic table and offer dry seating. As we munched on fresh fruit and trail mix, our conversation turned serious, and we were exploring some of the hard things we'd each faced growing up. That was when he mentioned the book that had made his view of his own life much easier to swallow: *The Road Less Traveled*, by M. Scott Peck. He shared the essence of a quote that stuck with him: that life is hard, and once you accept that life is hard the fact it is hard doesn't matter anymore.

We cut back across the same trail we had created, heading back to his car and the drive back to the city. I was more aware of the thoughts in my head than I was of the beauty that surrounded me. I couldn't let go of the meaning behind the quote: accepting that life is difficult was the key. We stopped at a bookstore on the way back and I bought my own copy of *The Road Less Traveled*. It became my reading material for the rest of that vacation.

Years later, when I met Kirk, we explored our pasts and their meaning. No topic was off limits. We showed a sincere respect for what the other had experienced. And… he'd read Peck's book.

We used a quotation from *The Road Less Traveled* in our wedding ceremony in 1989. A few years later, in 1994, I discovered that Peck was going to be in our area. We cut our workday short so that we would arrive well before the talk began. Seating was first come, first served, and we wanted to be as close to Peck as possible.

We entered the college's large auditorium that otherwise served as a basketball court. Hundreds of folding metal chairs squeaked and creaked as people tried to get comfortable. The room was alive with chatter. Kirk and I headed to the front and took two chairs along one aisle, so we'd have a clear sightline.

The room fell silent when Peck walked to the front. He appeared professorial, his eyes magnified by the lenses inside the clear, round frames of his glasses. I was surprised by his shyness, given the power and clarity of his writing. He had great difficulty making eye contact with members of the audience and his delivery was halting. However, he emphasized the concepts around self-discipline, delay of gratification, and his definition of real love—concepts that had resonated with my husband and I from the book. I was pleased we had come.

Peck's talk had triggered a painful memory for Kirk, and on the drive home he told me a story from when he was eight or nine. It was a late summer afternoon, and he was riding his bicycle through his neighborhood when something struck him and then wrapped around his neck. He nearly fell off his bike, stopping quickly and grabbing at whatever was causing this increasing pressure—when he saw that it was a live snake. He tore the snake from his neck, threw it to the ground, and then noticed some older boys standing, snickering, on the side of the road.

I heard the emotion in his voice and asked him if I could mirror him, using the communication technique first practiced when I attended a training on marital therapy that I now taught in my seminars.

Kirk didn't think the exercise was necessary as he was sure I'd understand, but I insisted.

"So, if I understand, you were embarrassed that you'd been the subject of a prank from those other boys."

"No," he said, "That's not it."

I paused, thinking about what he'd said in his story, and tried again.

"So, you were ashamed of your reaction, how you stopped quickly and threw the snake."

"No, that's not what I mean."

So, I asked Kirk to tell me the story again and I tried twice more unsuccessfully, not quite reflecting back to Kirk the deeper meaning behind his story.

I tried a fifth time. "So, if I understand you correctly, it was the fact that it was a live snake. You hate snakes, and you were more terrified of the snake than you were of the mean older boys."

"That's it!" Kirk said, sounding exhausted.

Several weeks later, we were on our way to meet friends for dinner.

The hour's drive gave us plenty of time to talk, and I had a few things to get off my chest.

Kirk kept his eyes on the road and his hands on the wheel as I started to share how hard it was to have a full-time job, cook all the meals, and try and keep the house clean. To do that, to get the house looking spick and span, took a series of chores and most of my Saturday. Then I'd turn around to find Kirk's clothing and things scattered about.

"I'd like to mirror you on this," Kirk said. "Is that okay?"

Since turnaround is fair play, I agreed, turning in the passenger seat to face him.

"If I get this, you're upset that you work so hard and I don't notice. Is that it?"

"No, I know you notice how hard I work. That's not it."

"Okay, let me try again. So, am I missing that you're resentful that Saturday is taken up with cleaning the house? Is that it?"

I said no again. He glanced over at me, little creases lining his forehead, and then back to the road.

"So, if I understand you, when you work so hard to clean the house and I leave my stuff lying around it makes you feel disrespected."

"Yes, Kirk, that's it." We began a discussion about how we could work together to better share the responsibilities around the house, and Kirk promised he'd try to be more careful with his things. I was relieved and felt supported, but more importantly, I felt understood.

Then I realized Kirk nailed my meaning in three attempts, and it took me five to get his... I—the trained psychotherapist—knew I had more work to do.

Between Kirk and I, that story of taking five times to find my husband's meaning, and it only taking him three to find mine, has become one of our inside jokes, funniest when we're in bed together reading before lights out. You'd think that, given my training, background, and experience as a therapist, I'd be able to nail it on the first try. Not so, apparently.

In the classes I taught at the retirement community, I'd use that story to illustrate how difficult it is to get to the core of what someone means.

Federal and state regulations required our employees to take classes centered on resident safety every year: topics like infection control, fire safety, preventing and reporting suspected resident abuse. Other required classes dealt with stress management, conflict resolution, and effective communication. Those were the classes that I taught.

One time I had to ask my teaching partner to take over my part of the class because I had a meeting I couldn't reschedule.

"Do you want me to teach your curriculum and use your examples, or shall I come up with some of my own?" she asked. It was a great question. Teaching the same subject but from a different angle was a great idea.

My meeting was over more quickly than I expected. Quietly stepping into the back of the room and ready to take over my part, I froze. I was transfixed by what my teaching partner was doing.

On a wide white board, she had drawn two ovals at the extremes of each side. The oval on the left represented person A, and the oval on the right was person B. Between the two ovals at the top of the board, she drew what looked like a coffee filter.

The class looked dazed until she gave an example. "What person A says isn't heard by person B the way it was meant."

She wrote the word gender below the illustration of the filter. "One filter that gets in the way of meaning is gender," she said. "Men and women, husbands and wives, often have conversations in which one person's meaning is clearly missed. Have any of you ever had that experience?"

The room erupted with laughter.

"My husband does not get my meaning, ever."

"Sometimes, I feel like I'm using a foreign language with my wife."

"Us not understanding each other? Happens on a daily basis."

"I can say the very same thing to my friend, and she gets it. But my husband? Not a chance."

My co-facilitator let the comments continue for a while, a smile broadening on her face.

"That's the point," she said. "We all have filters that sometimes make it very difficult to get someone else's meaning. Gender isn't the only one. What might some other filters be?"

Within five minutes the whiteboard was filled with words like race, education, job, birthplace, education, age, religion, wealth—or lack of it.

"So, what's the point?" She'd turned back to face the class.

One man raised his hand. "No wonder there are times when I'm talking, and the other person just doesn't get my meaning."

"Good," she said. "Now I'm going to have Yvonne take over and teach you a communication technique called mirroring. It can be very effective to help all of us cross the bridge to find someone else's meaning."

12

Mom Didn't Say

*M*y mom was one of the brightest women I knew. In the eighties, when I was in graduate school studying for my master's degree in clinical psychology, I had to take a mandatory class in tests and measurements which involved administering a variety of aptitude, intelligence, and personality assessments. For example, I was required to give the Weschler Intelligence Scale for Adults and my assignment was to give this test to a minimum of twenty individuals. I asked Mom if she'd be willing.

She was an easy subject. She thought the test was fun, manipulating the flash cards and puzzles, playing the word games, and doing the memory problems with joy. She even agreed to not knowing the results: her score was in the gifted range.

As the millennium came around twenty years later, Mom was a different person. Watching my mom slip into dementia, where her gifted-level intelligence either disappeared or was hiding, shook me. Even with all my experience—by that time—working with the elderly, I found it distressing to see her struggle to pull up the most basic memory.

Her morning ritual disappeared. No longer did she walk, coffee in hand, out to the mailbox to retrieve the daily paper for the daily crossword which, before dementia, she always completed before her second cup of coffee and breakfast. Those tidy letters filling all the squares were long gone, the paper untouched and front page still atop sitting idle unless Dad got around to reading it.

Her once-pristine flower beds went untended. The easy-to-maintain perennials kept the house looking beautiful in all seasons, but annuals were left un-weeded, untrimmed, unkempt. Mom was either in too much pain or too anxious to leave the house unless Dad was with her.

For a while she still recognized me and let me know she loved it when I'd visit. But Dad would share that there were moments when she'd ask, "Are we married?" Or "Do we have children?"

Her short-term memory was the first to go. Dad kept small cups of ice cream in the freezer and Mom would forget she'd eaten one, or two, or sometimes four in one day. She also began panicking if Dad left the room even for a moment, like to refill his coffee or go to the bathroom.

Mom and Dad had been sleeping in separate rooms for years. Mom complained of Dad's snoring; it was loud and deep almost to the point of shaking small objects sitting on the dresser. Dad complained that Mom rolled around too much, and that sometimes he'd wake up with her hand on his face or her knee in the middle of his back. Sleeping in separate rooms allowed them each more restful nights, neither having to wake if the other woke to pee.

That arrangement had worked well for them until the dementia took control. When Mom woke for the bathroom—sometimes two or three times a night—she'd go into Dad's bedroom and pull on his toes to see if he was still alive.

During weekly phone calls with Dad, he'd rant and rave about the latest disturbing thing Mom was doing, but he was absolutely committed to keeping her at home as long as she could take care of her own bathing, dressing, and teeth brushing.

A few weeks before Easter, 2002, I drove home for a visit. The front door of the split-level house opened onto stairs that led up to the living room, kitchen, and bedrooms. When I arrived, Mom was waiting for me, standing at the top of the landing in front of her organ, in the very spot I expected her to be. It was a glorious spring day, but Mom's smile when she saw me made the room glow even more. But when she hugged me, she felt fragile. The once comforting and affirming embrace was tentative, as if delivered or returned too tightly would cause her pain. Close up, beyond her smile, she appeared tired. Years of immediately fixing me something to eat the moment I arrived had changed. "Get yourself something to eat, then come down to the family room. I need to go and sit in my chair."

Her chair was a cushy gray-blue recliner with a heating pad strapped center-back that served as her sanctuary during her decline. Positioned near the gold brick fireplace, the chair was flanked by a table with a half-filled cup of coffee and a stack of unopened crossword puzzle books.

As I joined her with my sandwich, she was absorbed in a rerun of *Murder She Wrote* on television. I waited, knowing it was best to let her initiate any conversation to minimize her confusion.

"Yvonne."

I looked over. She was fixated on the stack of books.

"I can't do these anymore."

Something in her eyes told me there was more she wanted to say. I sat up straight and planted my feet on the floor, needing an anchor to the world I felt might be shifting under my feet.

She looked at me with dry eyes rimmed with deep sadness. "I want to go."

I swallowed my fear of losing her and the desire to tell her not to be silly, that she had many good years left, and said instead, "Tell me more, Mom. What do you mean?"

"I want to go. I'm always in pain. I don't do anything but sit here all day. I want to go."

I chose my words carefully. "I think I understand. You hurt all the time, you aren't gardening, you aren't going out, you're not doing the things you used to love to do. You're telling me you're ready." But I didn't feel ready.

One tear slipped from the corner of her eye. "I don't remember things. And I'm scared. I want to go."

I sat in silence a long time looking at her beautiful, pain-etched face. The ache around my heart began to fill the room. I prayed silently for wisdom while her eyes begged a response.

I went over to her chair, bent over and took her veined, papery hands in mine, being careful to keep my touch light. "It's okay with me. I will miss you like crazy. Talk to God. Let him know what you want."

After I left, Mom's behaviour deteriorated. Dad couldn't go anywhere without her screaming, "Mike, where are you?" The only way Dad could get her to settle was to scream back. She woke more frequently than before and neither of them was getting any sleep. Mom's doctor advised that she should be hospitalized—he wanted to monitor her while adjusting her meds and Dad would catch up on much-needed rest.

Dad called with the news and gave me the phone number in Mom's hospital room. When I called she began screaming. "Yvonne, get me out of here! I want to go home!"

A nurse took the phone from Mom and gently reassured me she'd handle the situation. The silence remaining on the line after the nurse hung up was deafening. Mom's high-pitched shriek reverberated through every cell of my body. I'd never witnessed her like that—livid and in a rage. She was always the epitome of politeness, bound by a strict code of controlled emotions and never any outbursts.

I shook as I hung up the phone, but I did not cry. I was totally helpless. My wonderful mom was in agony and there was nothing I could do.

I didn't call Dad—I didn't want him to have this on his plate as well. I clung to my belief that the hospital would help Mom quiet.

It hadn't been a month since my last visit home when Dad called in the early hours of the morning. I could hear the agony in his voice as he began to tell me Mom passed away during the night.

I was devastated. While I was relieved that Mom had been ready to go, and that she got what she wanted so quickly after she'd announced to me it was time, I was haunted. Had she wanted to die alone? In a hospital? How dare she? What would she want us to do? How did she want us to remember her? What did she want us to know?

I thought back to the conversation we had the month before. I was glad that I told her that I loved her and that I understood her wanting to go. I was honored that for once she wore her heart on her sleeve and told me her truth.

But still I was filled with a searing doubt. Our conversation happened when she was knee deep in the dementia. When she'd still been clear headed, what could I have done then? What should I have done then? What else might she have wanted me to know—if only I'd had the courage to ask? What truths was she holding inside her that would have answered these questions that kept niggling at me?

I knew there had to be something more. More meaningful for the person in their end-of-life journey. And more for those of us who remain—those responsible for honoring and in many cases guiding their departure. But what was it?

13

Annie's Dilemma

*W*hen I taught elementary school, I'd been privileged to teach six different levels of kids. When I moved to southeastern Pennsylvania I couldn't find a teaching job, but my master's degree in psychology provided the opportunity for me to counsel and train adults in an employee assistance program. But I'd never worked with the elderly, and I was interested.

When I received a call from the CEO of Frederick Living, a retirement community, asking me if I'd consider a position in human resources, I interviewed and was offered the job. My new position didn't offer me much in the way of direct contact with the residents, but it did give me the chance to work with and for the staff who did. It was here that I came face to face with end-of-life issues in a new way.

It was the start of a new century and I and other members of the ethics committee were seated at an oval table in the board room. A wall of windows made the room comfortable and bright, our pre-meeting chatter light and alive.

Our chaplain called the meeting to order and the look on his face immediately brought the temperature down in the room. The first order of business: Annie, a resident in the nursing wing with dementia who was incapable of speaking.

Annie's life was at risk because she'd developed a foot ulcer. Unless her foot was amputated, gangrene would develop and she'd die. The doctor had ordered whirlpool treatments and antibiotics, not only to save her leg but her life. Annie's daughter had medical power of attorney for healthcare decisions. That meant she could decide for her mother whether to allow the treatments based on her understanding of Annie's wishes. Annie had been adamant about her right to die, and she didn't want any life-prolonging treatments if her quality of life became diminished. Her daughter wanted to honor her mother's wishes by refusing the baths or the antibiotics.

The issue in front of the ethics committee was that Annie's advance directive had been created in another state which recognized quality of life as grounds for withholding treatment. Pennsylvania law had no such language, and Annie was now residing in Pennsylvania. The daughter was caught between what she thought her mother wanted and Pennsylvania state law.

Each member of the ethics committee had a say: we were filled with compassion for the situation, for Annie and for her daughter. And we had to follow the law. Our meeting ended with a way forward—a decision—but it wasn't a resolution to the matter at hand. So, with the daughter on one side of the decision and the ethics committee and the retirement community on the other, the case proceeded to court.

The court ruled within a matter of days that Annie was to have two surrogates. A court-appointed surrogate would allow the whirlpool and antibiotics, and if those treatments failed, the daughter would have the authority to refuse the amputation.

Instead of feeling relief, I felt numb. And full of new questions about the conversations I didn't have with Mom before she died. Although Mom's health had been in steady decline, no one would have guessed that, when she was admitted to hospital, she'd die suddenly in the middle of the night. Prior to her dementia, had she and Dad ever discussed what she might have wanted in the end? If they had, neither of them spoke about it to me. I'd been aware of this thing called advance directive, but I'd never initiated a discussion about them with either of my parents. If I had, I wondered, would it have made Mom's passing easier to bear?

Outside of work, I turned to thoughts of Dad. I had no idea whether he had any advance directives for himself. Even more disturbing, I realized that I had no idea what Dad might want.

My dismay soon turned to determination. In thinking about my father, the helplessness that I had felt in the past lifted as if it had never been there. There was something I could do, a way I could be helpful. It would require a little bit of research and perhaps several phone calls, but the most important call would be to Dad.

I found an attorney in Meadville that handled estates, wills, and advance directives. I arranged to take several days off to drive across the state and bring Dad to the meeting. The phone call telling him of my plans was a lot easier than I expected, but he did start the call with his usual gruffness.

"Dad, have you ever heard of a document called advance directive or a living will?" I held the phone away from my ear... just in case.

I was right to have been prepared. He was in the kitchen having finished his lunch; I could hear the tiny television on the shelf. He didn't turn it down, he yelled over it. "What in the hell are they?"

I shouted back: "It's a legal document that describes what kind of medical treatments you want at the end of your life."

I heard the ratty four-wheeled chrome and Naugahyde chair grind over the carpet. Dad turned off the television or lowered the volume. In a softer voice, he said, "What do you mean?"

"Well, if you have an attack of some kind, do you want to be resuscitated?"

"I guess it would depend on what kind of condition I'm in. If it looks like I won't have any quality of life, then hell, just let me go."

"That's exactly the point. If you don't have these documents, the medical folks would have to try and save you, no matter what."

"How d'you know this kind of stuff?" he asked.

I explained to him what I'd learned at the office and what he and I would have to do. I told him I'd already spoken to an attorney, and that I'd come to pick him up and together we'd get the process started.

The attorney's office was in one of the grand Victorian brick homes that gallantly lined the street not far from the center of Meadville. The day was chilly, hinting at the coming of winter. Inside it was bright with light and the attorney sat behind a desk covered with stacks of files.

She engaged in a little small talk, but quickly dove into the reason we had come. I could see that her frankness helped to settle Dad. She explained that what we were doing would in the end protect him and allow him to know that his desires as to medical treatment would be honored if he could no longer speak for himself. It would take a week or so to prepare the documents, and we arranged a date for the second meeting.

On our second meeting, the attorney went over the contents of the durable power of attorney for health care and authorizing refusal of medical treatment, and living will. The signing, witnessing, and notarization followed.

If I had expected to feel relief, it didn't happen. I knew this was the right thing to do but I was caught with the knowledge there might come a day when I'd have to authorize something that might potentially hasten his death. A tightness in my chest spread up through my throat and lingered during the ride back to Dad's house. The responsibility was an honor, but it was enormous. When the time came, would I have the strength to let him go when the medical system had the power to keep him alive?

14

Live Until You Die

I like to listen to National Public Radio. The programs still contain interruptions, but not as many as on commercial stations. And I'm a glutton for good storytelling.

One NPR story has stuck with me. It was a short piece, part of the evening news broadcast, about a newly formed grief counseling center for people who had suffered the loss of a pet. When we lose a human family member, others treat us with sensitivity and care. But that same compassion isn't always extended when it's a furry or feathered friend. Often, the narrator said, a pet is the only companion for a person who lives alone and the grief reaction of losing a pet is just as intense.

When the program ended, I felt like a ventriloquist's dummy—my head doing a 360-degree spin and, when it came back around, I had a totally different perspective. Whether grief comes from losing a pet, a partner, or facing our own impending death, we all need compassion and comforting.

As a psychotherapist, I'm required to complete continuing education every year to keep my state license. That long-ago NPR program sparked an interest in grief counseling and that's led me to take classes to deepen my skills.

During one such course, I hung back after the class to ask the instructor a question about Grace, one of my clients. As I walked up the narrow aisle flanked by long, cloth-covered tables, I wondered how to phrase a clear question. The room had emptied, save two people waiting in line ahead of me. I was grateful for the time to think.

I'd been seeing Grace off-and-on for twenty years. She'd often call, months and sometimes years since her last session, telling me it was time for a tune-up. While she was in college for her master's degree, Grace learned she had a congenital disease that explained the frequent illnesses that she had as a child. There was no cure, but medicines and surgery helped her to live a somewhat normal life—until they didn't any longer.

Grace and I would discuss her grief around the losses she experienced from her illness: daily limitations on places she could go, who she could see, and what she could do. I knew that I was her sounding board but, when her sessions ended, I often questioned whether I'd been any help to her at all.

When it was my turn to talk with the instructor, I gave him the background and revealed I had no idea how to be of more help to Grace. When I finished, he took a moment, the silence filling the huge lecture hall. Shortly, he looked directly into my eyes.

"The next time you see her, all you need to do is ask her one question."

"One question?" I was preparing for a much more complex and challenging recommendation from him. I was sure he'd tell me I needed more training, or that I'd been missing an important point, or even that I wasn't the right therapist for Grace any longer because I didn't think I was helping. I wasn't prepared for the simplicity of his ground-shifting, simple advice.

"Ask her how she wants to live until she dies."

"That's it?"

"Yes. Isn't that at the core of her struggle?"

All through the rest of the conference and on the drive home, the question echoed in my head.

"How do you want to live until you die?"

Months later, Grace called again. Her kidney transplant had failed, she was back on dialysis, but miraculously she became a candidate for another transplant. She was on massive doses of anti-rejection drugs and dealing with the awful side effects. Her depression was back with a vengeance.

I listened, validated, and handed her a box of tissues as she told her story. All the while the question was rattling in my head, my unease growing. Was it so simple? During the next pause in Grace's sharing, I said, "Grace, I have what may seem like a strange question for you. Are you ready for it?"

She nodded, her lips still trembling, tears staining her face red. With a trepidation I hoped she wouldn't notice, I sat up a little straighter, planted my feet on the floor, and gazed directly at her.

"How do you want to live until you die?"

Grace started to laugh, exploding the tension I'd been holding. It was the hearty belly laugh of hers that I so enjoyed. "That's the best question you have asked me in a long, long time. How do I want to live until I die? Well, I surely will have to think about that."

Grace came in for several more tune-ups after that. She was usually upset with her life. Even with her limitations, she wasn't living the life she wanted. I'd use the question to guide our discussions. "So how do you want to live until you die?"

The minute the question came out of my mouth, she would look up and smile.

Finally, in one session, she had an answer. "I want to have a purpose; I want to do something that has meaning."

"What does that look like to you?"

"I want to do something that's helpful to others."

We set to work on a list of things that would be helpful to others and were possible for her, given her physical limitations. When that was finished, I said, "Good, now here's your homework. Take a couple of days to think about one thing from your list that you'll do in the next two weeks. Call me once you've decided."

She did. She began at her church, answering the phones and handling other administrative duties.

At each tune-up something similar happened. We'd explore her list, she'd make a selection, and implement her choice following our session.

The focus of our sessions began to turn from her expressions of despair to lighter conversations around what she was learning about herself and the value she could still bring to others despite her health limitations.

And I no longer watched her walk out the door wondering if I had been helpful.

Most of us don't ask ourselves, or our loved ones, how we want to live until we die. Even when we do, we rarely include the final part about how we want to transition from life—how we want to leave life.

How do we want to live until we die?

How do we want to live as we die?

How do we want to leave life?

15

Meeting Mary

*C*onstruction of the brand new personal-care building took several years instead of the planned year and a half. I'd finally be able to give up my tiny cubicle in the trailer parked on the property. At a meeting to determine who would be assigned to which new office, someone suggested that my administrative assistant and I should be on the first floor near the receptionist's desk.

I said I'd prefer to be in a less open, less congested part of the building. If employees wanted to see me about something sensitive and private, I didn't want them to have to worry about being seen coming into or out of my office. I was delighted that my reasoning was accepted, and I was assigned an office on the third floor near the elevator but beyond inquisitive eyes.

My office proved to be the right one for a different reason. While employees didn't usually pass my office, residents did. If they were returning to their apartments after a meal or a presentation in the auditorium, they'd walk right past my door. Because I kept it open, some would stop by and say hello or ask a question. Residents and their needs were a priority for all employees. We were expected to drop whatever we were doing whenever approached with a request from them. I relished the opportunity to get to know at least a few.

On one snowy evening, as it neared time for me to go home, a resident stopped at the door and asked, "Can you come with me quickly?"

"Of course," I replied, getting up out of my chair. I was curious.

"I need to show you something," she said, pushing her walker ahead of her. "We'll have to hurry." I chuckled quietly at the odd juxtaposition and then worked to keep up with her short, steady, and surprisingly quick steps.

We reached her apartment and she allowed me to open the door for her. With more expert coordination of her walker and feet, she moved to the large picture window that faced due west. "Look," she said, so close to the window her breath left a trace of fog on the pane. "I didn't want to experience this alone. I had to share it with someone, and you seemed like the right person."

There in front of us was one of the most brilliant sunsets I had ever seen. The lavender, purple, magenta, and fuchsia sky was doubly magnificent as it reflected off the snow on the ground. I looked at the woman, the smile on her face as vivid as the sky, as she reached across the left bar of her walker to take my hand. We needed no conversation. We stayed like that until darkness blanketed her little apartment.

She went over to a side table and turned on the light. "Thank you," she said, turning to face me. "I'm Mary. Somehow, I had a feeling you'd see what I was seeing."

And so began our relationship. Mary would often invite me to her apartment. On top of her desk were some cherished mementos of her life with her husband. He had carved folk art figures that had been part of a Pennsylvania Dutch farm scene. People from miles around would come to see the diorama that he created with its workers, animals, and farm equipment. While most had been sold at auction, Mary kept several favorites. These carved pieces would trigger conversations about major events in her life. How she met her husband, how they'd adopted two children, the wonderful house her husband built, their gardens and fruit trees. She shared the sorrow of losing both her son and husband, and how much she appreciated that she still had her daughter.

For me, my relationship with Mary exemplified one of the joys of working with the elderly: she was full of history. She lived in Washington DC during WWII, and she had worked for a war intelligence agency. She still couldn't talk about her work there.

She told me about Eleanor Roosevelt. Mary's church group was invited to the White House to perform Christmas carols for Mrs. Roosevelt and some of the house staff. She watched two of the Roosevelt children slide down the banister before the concert. The evening ended with Mrs. Roosevelt serving them all cookies and hot chocolate.

Mary was equally interested in my life and would revel in what she called my "adventures." She was a golden human who filled an empty space for me—that of a grandparent.

As is a given for us all, Mary started on a steady physical decline. She spent most of her days sitting in her apartment. She'd be sitting in the comfy, overstuffed chair in the right corner near the window in her living room. Often, with no lights on. Our once-easy conversations became difficult: I'd ask questions but receive one-word answers. Many times, I'd simply sit in silence with her until the heaviness in the room told me that it was time to go.

Perhaps a year after my retirement, I received news that Mary was in the nursing unit receiving hospice care. When I arrived, the director of nursing approached me so that I could be prepared; Mary was unresponsive and in a coma.

I stood outside of her room and did some deep breathing, silently reciting my favorite prayers. In hospice training, we'd been taught to bring something with us to help pass the time. Since Mary had shared her deep connection to the church, I had a Bible in hand.

Mary was in the single bed nearest the door—the privacy curtain pulled closed. She smelled like fresh soap, her skin remarkably smooth and unlined, her face expressionless. But it was her hair that made me take a step back. Mary would have been appalled. Instead of waves, one stacked on top of the other framing her face, someone had combed her hair straight back and unparted.

Hospice training also taught me to introduce myself and to act and speak as though in normal conversation. I took the chair beside her. "Hi Mary, it's Yvonne," I said, as though she was dozing. "It's a beautiful day outside, the sky is blue, and the sun is shining. I've brought you something." My hand dropped to the Bible resting on my lap.

I opened it to the bookmark I'd placed in the Book of Psalms. I'd chosen them because I thought Mary would enjoy them. I read for perhaps a half an hour, pausing between each psalm to make a comment. "It's soothing to have the psalmist describe a good man like a tree planted beside a stream." I read only those psalms that were filled with delight, the wonders of nature, or that expressed a positive affirmation. I wanted the air in the room to be filled with light and warmth.

Again, I was doing what I wanted. Or what I thought she wanted. Again, deep inside me that seed of end-of-life conversations was palpable, but when would it germinate?

I continued my visits every day, and the scene was the same. Perhaps on the third or fourth visit, Mary's nurse told me she was glad to see me because, on her shift, I was Mary's only visitor.

My husband and I had planned a vacation. I shared with Mary where I was going and when I would return. I told her that I would come back with stories of adventure. I said goodbye, knowing full well I might never see her again.

When I arrived home, there was a voicemail asking me to call one of the nursing staff members. I knew without making the call that Mary had passed away. There was a soft crack in my chest.

Mary's journey was over, but in the space of the crack was a warmth. Mary and I had shared those priceless end-of-life moments. What I wished for Mary was that she'd been able to share deeper end-of-life conversations with her loved ones—someone other than me.

16

Walking with Winnie

$\mathcal{I}$ noticed a tiny woman, not much taller than five feet, walking down the hall in the nursing unit. There was an unmistakable, elegant strength about her. She was so chic that I turned and watched her until she turned the corner and was no longer in view. I began to see her often.

She was always dressed as though she were on her way to work. She wore an A-line wool skirt with a matching long-sleeved sweater. Gracing her neck was either a string of pearls or a French rope gold necklace. Her skirts always came just below her knees. Her low-heeled pumps matched her outfit. Her hair was her crowning glory, always impeccably coiffed, piled neatly on top of her head, held in place by tortoiseshell hair combs. She stood and walked with the grace of a ballerina.

She was ninety-eight years old. Her name was Winnie and we were soon talking as if we had been next door neighbors who shared lazy afternoons having tea and conversation on the front porch.

She and her husband, Logan, had owned a jewelry store. They started the business during the depression because Logan had a talent for repairing watches. While there were plenty of watches needing fixing, the income didn't stretch, partly because many customers couldn't pay. There were many months when Winnie worried how they would afford the coal they needed to stay warm.

It was a quirky, serendipitous incident that prompted their business to blossom. A man walked into the store and plunked several pieces of jewelry and a handful of watches onto the counter that stood between him and Winnie and Logan. He said that, if they could sell the pieces for him, he'd split the proceeds.

Everything sold and Logan was able to get a loan to purchase more jewelry to sell. It was the start of a prosperous business that developed a sterling reputation. Logan didn't feel comfortable choosing jewelry to be sold, nor did he like interacting with customers. He knew the business could expand, but he wanted to remain with what he loved, behind the scenes and repairing watches. Winnie took on the jewelry sales and customer service side of the business. She traveled to find the perfect pieces to bring in and sell, and soon expanded their product line to include fine china.

As much as I was fascinated with Winnie's life and travels, she was equally interested with mine. She always pumped me on my latest endeavor or escapade, even when something went wrong. I recognized early on that this was another grandmother I never had. Three of my grandparents had died before I was born, and my surviving grandmother had been emotionally unable to play the part.

Like my mom and dad, and everyone's mother or father, Winnie had a life filled with, well, life.

With young children, there are many adults around to welcome them and be part of their journey—hence the fairy godmothers. Winnie had people who had been part of her magical life. Now, because I worked in the building she lived in, I had been invited into that life, but the people who had been around her were either gone from this world or absent from her world for other reasons. Even with family around, if those family members weren't comfortable with end-of-life conversations, then how could they take place? And who would have end-of-life conversations with all the other Winnies? How might the future look for those of us who did not have family, or whose families were thousands of miles away? Could there be a new type of godmother that could guide the elders?

Over time, Winnie's eyesight faded. She gave up reading, her greatest enjoyment. We tried recorded books, but she was unable to manage the buttons on the device. For most of the day, she sat in the silence of her room. When I went to visit, I would find her in the Queen Anne chair to the left of the picture window. Each time I'd arrive, her face lit up. "Pull up the stool," was her greeting.

I loved my place at her knees.

I was invited to her 100th birthday celebration where she was surrounded by five generations of her family. The room was alive with stories. Toddlers scooted across the floor, and adults gathered around her in conversation. The center of attention, Winnie was radiant.

But these kinds of celebrations for those who reach these milestones are not always conducive to discussions about the intersection between life and death. They are not intimate in a one-on-one, be-my-health-care-agent way.

As time passed, more and more of her friends at the retirement community died. Winnie began to speak frequently of feeling the lack of purpose in her life and the loneliness that came with it. Time stretched ahead of her like a heavy blanket, and she started to talk about wanting to die.

The first time she said something to me about it, I wanted to say, "Don't say that. Don't even think that. I can't imagine not having you around." But these words remained locked inside. Reflecting on my reaction allows me to see how we are socialized to reject those comments—which certainly curtails deep discussions.

Instead, I leaned into her and took her hand and asked her to tell me more.

"Logan is gone. My friends are gone. I sit here all day looking forward to the phone call with my daughter, but even that isn't enough anymore. I just want to go."

I listened, and validated, listened, and validated.

When Winnie reached her 103rd birthday, she celebrated it sitting in the chair in her living room in her nightgown. Aides had taken over doing her hair, and though they tried to do it her way, it never had the same polished look as those earlier years—when she was 98, 99, and into her early 100s.

More and more often when I visited, she'd be in bed. She had made it clear that if I came into the room and she was asleep, I was to wake her. She wanted me to talk. There was no story too mundane or small. I tried to find something that would make her smile or laugh, and I was often successful. I was always prepared to listen to her say she wanted to go.

It wasn't too long after her 103rd that my phone rang at two in the morning. It was Winnie's daughter calling from Maine. Her voice shook as she told me that the aides had come in to check on her mother, finding her on the floor of the bathroom. Winnie was gone.

I told her daughter that I would go in. I would stay with Winnie until the undertaker arrived. I threw on a pair of jeans and a sweater and headed out of the house. I stopped at the nurses' station to let them know of my arrival.

One of the aides stepped in front of me, opened her arms, and enfolded me while I sobbed in a way my inner child would in losing her loving grandparent. When the tears subsided, she asked, "Are you ready to go in? Do you want me to come along?" I shook my head. I was ready to go alone.

I entered Winnie's quarters and went straight into the bedroom. She was lying on the bed, her gleaming white hair pulled straight back from her forehead, streaming behind her head and laying gently on her shoulders. Her face was still, and her eyes were closed. The light on the bedside table reflected off her porcelain skin. I sat and began to stroke her face and hands, speaking to her spirit.

Eventually, the funeral home attendant arrived, placing Winnie in a black body bag and shifting her to a gurney.

"I want to walk out with you," I said to the attendant. "She shouldn't have to leave here alone."

How did I know that's what she wanted? It's what I wanted. It's what I thought she would have wanted. The topic of end-of-life wishes weighed heavily in the background of my future intentions. What did I want?

My body collapsed into the driver's seat of my car. I was exhausted. Afraid I might fall asleep at the wheel, I turned on the only kind of music that would keep me awake—country.

As I rounded the corner of the township park, the light of the full moon was bouncing off the lake. I was taken by the ethereal beauty of it all. Seeing something moving, I slowed down to watch one lone Canada goose fly across the face of the moon. Martina McBride was singing the song, "Anyway," which is about feeling the pain and doing it anyway, living life anyway.

It took the goose forever to cross the sky, and as it did, Winnie's voice rang out to me. She was telling me what our conversations together had meant to her. She said her heart was full of my listening to the sorrows and joys in her life. She told me how proud she was of who I was and who I would continue to become. She was giving me my marching orders to continue to love expansively, to work with purpose and meaning, and to dream and find the next adventure.

She was saying goodbye for now, and she was saying that even when life gets difficult, I should do what I know is right.

17

A Gift to the Family

While working at the retirement community, I'd often find myself in the office of our national health administrator, a seasoned professional with the huge responsibility of overseeing the personal and nursing care of the residents. State and federal governments regulate this care and part of her job was to complete yearly surveys to show we were following the regulations. She therefore managed, monitored, and mentored the staff, documenting the work they completed to make later verification by regulators easier.

Overloaded bookshelves in her office reflected the sizeable responsibility and wealth of knowledge her position required: manuals, guides, and lawbooks detailing all the relevant regulations at both the state and federal level.

The office itself was tiny, which probably explained the stacks of paperwork on her desk and piles of folders on the floor. A master of controlled chaos, she knew exactly what was in each pile and could retrieve whatever she needed within seconds.

Despite the clutter, her office was one of the most welcoming in the building. She had adorned her two windows with brightly colored valances. The walls wore cheerful country prints and plaques with her favorite inspirational and motivational sayings.

But it was the woman herself that made it so comfortable. Businesslike when called for, she was deeply warm and engaging. Laughter often spilled from her office and warmed the reception area.

It was 2006. Mom was four years gone and Dad was in poor health. The director of nursing and I were in the tiny office of the amazing administrator, the three of us discussing a minor staff problem. Somehow the discussion changed to advance directives. The administrator's face lit up. She almost fell over as she stretched then reached under a stack of papers and pulled out a substantial blue and white booklet.

"It's called the Five Wishes," she said, holding the booklet in the air between us. "It can be used as both legal power of attorney and advance directive, but it does much more. It covers things that are essential to think about at the end of life, beyond medical treatment."

Her soft blue eyes dropped to the booklet as she opened it and turned to the middle section. "Look, people choose how they want things to be." She flipped a few more pages, then continued.

"Listen to this: I wish to have my family, friends, and others know that I forgive them for when they may have hurt me in my life. And this one: I wish for family and friends to know that I do not fear death. I think it is not the end but a new beginning for me."

She closed the booklet and slid it across the desk. "I won't read the rest of it to you, but it's filled with important emotional and spiritual things we really should be talking about with our families. I have extra copies if you'd like to borrow one."

I stood and gestured toward the booklet, my palm open toward the ceiling as if I had just realized I was being given a sacred and wonderful gift. She looked directly into my eyes as she handed me the booklet. "I knew you'd be interested. Let me know what you think."

I walked back to my office, curious yet mildly annoyed. Annoyed because Dad and I had completed his advance directive and medical power of attorney, and I'd thought we'd taken care of what was important. I felt an inch or so of resentment that I'd have yet another thing to do. But I was intrigued. I wondered how Dad would respond to some of the intimate statements I'd heard.

I laid the booklet on my desk and answered the ringing phone. I was needed immediately somewhere else in the facility, so off I went. As frequently happened, other letters, paperwork, and forms ended on top of something I wanted to act on. In this case, the Five Wishes® booklet. I forgot all about it.

I can stand clutter and disorganization for only so long. It was Friday and the other third-floor employees had left for the weekend. It was as good a time as any to make some sense of the top of my desk. And I had an ulterior motive: housekeeping would be in over the weekend and unless I cleared the top of my desk, it wouldn't get cleaned.

I filled the recycling basket, returned files to their rightful spots, and placed documents ready for the signature of others in my outbox. Suddenly, there it was, popping out at me: the Five Wishes® booklet.

It was as if I were seeing it for the very first time. The cover listed the contents of each wish: who would make care decisions if I couldn't, the kind of medical treatment I would or wouldn't want, what would make me comfortable, how I wanted to be treated, and what I wanted my loved ones to know.

My curiosity about the last three got the better of me and I sat down and began to read. I sat at my desk for over an hour reading section by section, sometimes reading a section twice.

Wanting to know more, I turned to my computer. The founder of the Five Wishes®, Jim Towey, a licensed attorney, had met Mother Teresa in Calcutta when he worked for Oregon Senator Mark Hatfield. She asked him to visit a home where her volunteers treated the sick and dying, requesting he clean one man's bedsores. Towey has said that he was initially reluctant to touch the man, but the experience changed him. He discovered a deep compassion for the man, which then extended to the poor and the dying, realizing they deserved to have a louder voice in determining how they wished to be treated in their final days.

When he returned to Washington, he volunteered in a soup kitchen and in another of Mother Theresa's homes, this one for people with AIDS. He worked as Mother Teresa's legal counsel to prevent the unauthorized use of her image and her name. And he went on to work for the Department of Health and Rehabilitative Services in Florida, and for the federal government under President George W. Bush.

Mr. Towey wanted to create a way for families to manage and cope when a loved one was facing a serious illness or death. So he established a non-profit organization, Aging with Dignity. He authored the original Five Wishes®, and it had received the help of medical experts and a commission of the American Bar Association in 1996.

The Five Wishes® document is now recognized in at least forty-six US states as an advance directive. Even in the remaining few states where the Five Wishes® may not be legally recognized, it can still be useful when completed and attached to other documents, such as an advance directive, that are legal in the jurisdiction.

Sitting at my desk that late Friday afternoon, I was struck by the juxtaposition of the legal weight of the Five Wishes® document when it didn't have an ounce of legalese wording in it. Anything and everything that needed to be considered was laid out in plain language.

Millions of copies in many languages, even braille, have been distributed by more than 40,000 organizations: health care systems, hospitals, hospices, financial planners, and estate planners. I read that Samaritan, a hospice care provider, calls the Five Wishes® "a gift to the family, friends and the doctors of the loved one," because it doesn't put them into the awkward position of having to guess what kind of treatment the person wants or doesn't want. In 2011, Aging with Dignity also published an online version.

I dug deeper. And I thought some more.

The Five Wishes® are like advance directives with heart and soul. Like an advance directive document, it covers naming a person to make medical decisions if the person writing the document can no longer do so for reasons of physical or intellectual incapacity. It also lists the kind of medical treatments that the person does or does not want, and under what conditions.

But unlike other advance directives, the Five Wishes® addresses other issues. In the wish of how comfortable one wants to be, some items are: not wanting to be in pain, help in cases of suspected depression, being kept fresh and clean, having religious or spiritual readings when near death. In the wish of how one wants to be treated by everyone, for example: children, caregivers, friends and loved ones. Preferences of having people around, specifics like having someone hold their hand, and philosophical choices such as to act with kindness and cheerfulness and not sadness or pity. Through the Five Wishes®, family and friends of the loved one who is dying are able to receive messages such as: they are loved, they are forgiven, they are wished peace.

Each wish goes into further detail. If there's something the person chooses not to have, something they consider unimportant, or which goes against a particular belief, like organ donation for example, they can simply cross it out.

When I finished my exhaustive search and study session, I turned off my computer and stood up, preparing to come out from behind the desk. But I had to stop and put my head in my hands, suddenly overwhelmed. The beauty and awfulness of it all lay like a rock in the center of my chest.

If I could do this with Dad, if I pushed through the fear of broaching the subject, I'd be able to touch the heart and soul of the man I longed to know better. If I could do it, he'd know that his thoughts and desires about what was important to him were being placed in my hands to treasure and to honor. He'd be saying, "I trust you with all of this.

When the end comes, I trust that you will do what is most important for me."

If I could do it...

18

There is No Try

$\mathcal{T}$he blue and white eleven-page booklet lay on the passenger seat beside me. For whatever reason, I wanted it to be where a sideways glance would remind me of the priorities I'd set for the next several days. I willed it to give me strength on the six-and-a-half-hour drive back to Dad's house; hoped it would nudge me to do what I strongly believed was necessary.

I had taken my all-wheel drive car into the dealership for a travel inspection and, to be on the safe side, fluids were topped up, tires rotated and pressure checked, and hoses inspected for leaks. These, plus an oil and filter change, gave me a much-needed sense that the car was winter roadworthy.

I checked the weather forecast and the driving conditions the night before leaving. Although there had been heavy snowfall several days before, the roads were supposed to be clear and dry all the way. Still, I like to be prepared just in case, and my car was packed with a mylar blanket, a sleeping bag, food, and water for several days, audiobooks to keep me company, and, of course, my cross-country ski equipment.

A blanket of white under gray skies gave the passing miles the stillness to do what I knew I needed to do: think. I wanted the Five

Wishes® to be complete by the time I headed back home. My biggest concern was how to introduce them to Dad. Since we'd already done his advance directive, would he balk at having to do something similar?

I imagined his familiar deep, sharp tone and that he'd say something like, "What the hell do we need to do now? I thought this was all settled." Then I'd stand there feeling like my ten-year-old self. Depending on my mood and how insignificant I felt, I might back down.

The more I wrestled with what to do, I kept coming back to one thing. I needed to monitor his mood. But I'd eventually have to jump in feet first and tell him why I thought it was important to do this.

I headed straight to the hospital when I arrived in Meadville. The pewter sky was beginning to turn an inky black, which matched my apprehension. The hospital smells hit me the moment I stepped through the sliding glass door. The halls were quiet, but the food trollies told me that I had come at supper time.

When I entered Dad's room, I greeted his roommate and walked past the privacy curtain. I was pleased Dad's bed was near the huge window that took up most the width of the wall—a view and natural light, even though it was evening, would help to buoy his mood and it definitely helped reinforce mine.

He was sitting up in his bed, dinner all done. He looked up and broke into the impish grin I knew so well. "Hi hon. I was wondering when you would get in." He glanced over to the empty tray and its plates. "Looks like you planned it well. It's good to see you. How was the drive?"

Something inside me broke with relief. We were starting on a high note. I answered his question, and we talked about what had landed him in the hospital this time. His blood sugar had been out of whack and the doctor wanted to try and adjust his medications. Things had begun to stabilize and he was feeling much better.

While I was listening intently, I was also saying a little prayer for heavenly guidance. I came right to the point. "Hey Dad, do you remember going to the attorney's office and doing the advance directive?"

"Yeah, why?"

"Well, I learned recently that there is another document that covers information that isn't in the one we did with the attorney. Are you up for taking a look at it now?"

"Sure," he said as he swung his legs over the side of the bed. He patted the place beside him, and I took his dinner tray and set it on the windowsill. I lowered his hospital table so that I could write, and I sat down beside him. The spot was still warm from him.

I showed him the cover which listed the contents. I took my finger and traced down the list of things in the Five Wishes®. I explained that the first two wishes were the same as those in the advance directive: who could make medical decisions for him if he couldn't; and the kind of medical treatment he wanted or didn't want. The last three wishes were different. They covered how comfortable he wanted to be, how he wanted people to treat him, and what he wanted his loved ones to know. We settled in and went item by item.

We started with Wish One: the person I want to make health care decisions for me when I can't make them for myself. He named me as his health care agent with my sister and my brother listed as alternates if I became unavailable.

Light-hearted sarcasm began to flow over some of the items. He looked at me once with a glint in his eye and said, "Better be careful from now on, I can revoke these awesome privileges I'm giving you."

We were going through the list of what he wanted me, his health care agent, to do, but when it came to donating his organs he said, "Cross that out. I can't imagine mine would be worth much to anyone. Hell, I'm old and diabetic."

"Got it," I said as I drew a line through the item. When we came to the end of the list he paused and turned to me, and I wrote his exact words in the space provided. "If there is a 75 percent chance to live with quality of life, okay. I don't want to be a vegetable and have you kids suffering along with me."

The life support section came next, and it was harder for me than it seemed for him. He didn't want anything done if he was close to death, in a coma, or permanently or severely brain damaged. He said again, "If there's not a strong possibility of surviving and having quality of life, none of the life support measures listed above."

He agreed to every item listed in the section of how comfortable he wanted to be and how he wanted people to treat him. He said that my siblings and I could choose the readings for the funeral service, but he named two that were meaningful to him, the 23rd Psalm and the last stanza of Thanatopsis. He had memorized the poem when he was in grade school, and he would quote it now and then. This time I hung on every word as he repeated it from memory.

> *So live, that when thy summons comes to join*
> *The innumerable caravan, which moves*
> *To that mysterious realm, where each shall take*
> *His chamber in the silent halls of death,*
> *Thou go not, like the quarry-slave at night,*
> *Scourged to his dungeon, but, sustained and soothed*
> *By an unfaltering trust, approach thy grave,*
> *Like one who wraps the drapery of his couch*
> *About him, and lies down to pleasant dreams.*

My heart flooded and I kept the tears from spilling down my cheeks when he talked about how he wanted to be treated. He wanted people with him, his hand held, people praying for him, being kept clean if his bowels or bladder failed, and he wanted to die at home if that was possible. He turned and looked at me, his eyes wide, showing both amazement and pleasure, "Geez, these guys have thought of everything."

I reminded myself to keep breathing as we covered the last section

—what he wanted his loved ones to know. We were openly talking about things we had never discussed before. He wanted us to know he loved us, and that he was sorry if he'd ever done anything to hurt us. He wanted us to remember him when he was vibrant and in good health.

When I asked if there was anything he wanted to be remembered for, he paused and was silent for a moment, "I suppose working with the Red Cross and the emergency response team."

"What about your service in the war?" I asked, surprised his time as a B24 navigator hadn't come up.

"Well, I suppose that too." He looked at me with those deep brown eyes and they started to twinkle. "I want to be remembered as a man who loved a good joke."

He rattled off exactly what his funeral was to be. "I want you and Kirk to sing the 'Lord's Prayer,' 'Amazing Grace,' and the 'Ave Maria.' I'd like the 'Air Force Hymn' if that would be allowed."

He finished with something that I'd heard many times before, but it took on new meaning that day.

"I want to be carried feet first out of the house."

As I was about to leave the room to find the two witnesses that we needed to witness his signature, one of Dad's dear friends walked through the door, the flowing white beard I'd remembered from his days playing Santa Claus for the Thanksgiving Day parade in Meadville gone from his sweet face. He shaved his beard every Christmas Day and would start to grow it again each May. Now, he was clean shaven—no more playing Santa.

I asked him if was willing to be a witness. He was pleased to oblige. We still needed one more witness, so I went to the nurse's station where I found a volunteer. Dad's friend and the volunteer watched Dad pick up my pen with his stubby fingers. There was the tiniest bit of waver, but the signature was clear and precise: Michael Caputo. His friend wanted to stay and visit. I was hungry and tired yet elated. I wanted something to eat—anything—and I wanted to be alone.

I didn't know whether I wanted to dance or sing or cry. But we had done it, and in a way that Dad wanted. A simple yet profound twelve-page, blue-and-white document called the Five Wishes® had been the road map I needed. The completed Five Wishes® document was in my hands. I now had everything I'd need to honor my dad's wishes if called upon to make the ultimate decision for my father. As difficult as it had been to walk into the hospital, the trepidation was worth every step.

As I walked out of the hospital on that heady evening, I considered the design of the Five Wishes® booklet: soft blue, much like that of a pristine afternoon sky; the white letters of the title distinct against the background; the dark blue letters over white numbers making it clear as to the document's contents. Inside, the document is the same. The blue lettering easy to read. The choice of color was fitting, I thought. Blue represents both spirituality and serenity, which was exactly what I felt when I had the completed document in hand.

Dad and I had accomplished something of real importance. We had connected on a deeper level, a spiritual plane, in a way we hadn't ever before.

19

Feet First

*T*he hospital seemed to be Dad's favorite place to be around the Christmas holidays. It was 2009. This was perhaps his fourth hospital stay over the holidays since Mom had passed in 2002. The first three times, he needed his blood sugars to stabilize, but this time he couldn't keep food down. Even when there was nothing left, he kept having dry heaves.

So, the day after Christmas, Kirk and I packed up the car to head back to Meadville to see Dad. Kirk and his brother, Skip, were in the front, sharing the driving. Skip had come from Montana to spend the holidays with us and had agreed to join us for the trip to Meadville.

When we entered the room, Dad greeted us with a broad grin. He grabbed the TV remote and turned the sound down. He was feeling much better: his dry heaves had resolved, he was eating again and keeping the food down, and the pain across his upper back was being managed with medicines. But he wasn't out of the woods yet. Doctors wanted to keep him a few more days.

Kirk, Skip, and I stayed at Dad's house, making sure it was spick-and-span, the laundry done, and groceries put away for when he returned home. We visited Dad at the hospital twice daily. Our last visit was a morning visit, Kirk and Skip saying their goodbyes then leaving to get the car gassed up while I had some time alone with Dad. I wanted to give him the first draft of the book I'd written about his experiences getting into World War II as a B24 navigator and his tour of duty overseas. It was an early version of the book that would become *Flying With Dad*.

I sat on the edge of the bed and read several of my favorite chapters to him. I wanted the comfortable warmth that spread between us to last forever. We had always found it difficult to talk about things that really mattered. But my asking, and his telling me of his WWII stories, had allowed him to share his life and his soul with me. I had come to understand who he was and why he behaved in the ways that he had. In return, he had come to know me in the way I had always craved. We'd come so far as father and daughter.

The magic of the moment vanished when my cell phone rang. Kirk and Skip were ready and waiting in the car for the drive to the other side of the state. I closed the burgundy binder and put it into Dad's hands. There was one more thing I wanted him to know.

"Dad, I am so proud of you for your service during the war."

"For heaven's sake," Dad said with his usual bluster. Then, more softly he continued, "I'm proud of you. You wrote the book." His face was soft and serious.

We said our goodbyes. On the way out of the hospital I almost collided with a mother and daughter as I rounded the corner into the lobby. I was oblivious to anything except his words: "I'm proud of you."

My seat in the back of the car became like a cocoon. I was wrapped in the love that I experienced coming from Dad through those words. The long trip wasn't long at all. When we pulled into the driveway at home the house seemed different. The Christmas decorations were still up and, when we turned the tree lights on, I relished in the glowing gift I had been given by Dad.

THE SPELL WAS BROKEN THE FOLLOWING DAY WHEN THE PHONE RANG. I picked up the receiver to hear Dad screaming at me. "Why in the hell did you tell the hospital that I could go home?" I pulled the receiver away from my ear. "They sent me home with no pain medication. I'm in agony."

I steadied myself and tapped into a place of calm. "I told the hospital that you could go home when you were ready. It certainly doesn't sound as if you're ready."

His next words, in an uncharacteristic near whisper, shook me. "Yvonne, I'm scared. Can you come home?"

"Of course. I'll take a leave of absence and I can stay as long as you need me."

While this immediately calmed him, I knew what needed to be done and I didn't think Dad was going to be happy about it. I said it anyway. "Dad, you can no longer live alone. We're going to have to go to plan B."

"I know."

"I'll make some phone calls. I'll find someone to stay with you tonight and until I can get home. It's too late for me to leave now, but I'll be there as soon as I can tomorrow."

"Yvonne, I'm sorry I yelled at you." Over the years, I'd lost count of the times Dad had yelled at me, at all us kids. Not once that I could remember had he ever apologized for it. I didn't know whether to be grateful—or more worried about him.

I spent the next several hours making phone calls to get things settled. My left ear was raw. My final call was to Dad to tell him that someone was on the way to stay with him. An old friend's granddaughter was a nurse's aide who was willing to spend the night.

I set out early the next day. Thank God Pennsylvania didn't restrict talking on the phone while driving. I called Dad several times to see how he was doing. I called the hospital and the pharmacy. A prescription was waiting, and Dad's nurse's aide would be able to pick it up and take it to him.

Mid-afternoon, I called Dad again. I could immediately tell he was feeling better, and his words were like manna from heaven. "The medicine has taken away most of the pain and, by the way hon, this young woman is just what the doctor ordered. She came in and took charge."

A wave of relief spilled all over me. I was driving through a valley, rolling hills all around me. The bare trees were peeking up tall and stark from under a blanket of snow. The gray skies mirrored my mood, and I burst into tears.

My dear friend, Barb, greeted me at the door. She'd come to relieve her granddaughter, who had to go to work. She nodded toward the kitchen. Dad called to me—I didn't recognize his voice. Gone was the confident bark to be replaced by something that sounded like it had been through the wringer. I left Barb at the door and went to check on him. He was seated in the Naugahyde chair. As he pushed away from the little table that was attached to the wall, his look communicated the pain he'd been in all night.

"I'm glad you're home. The medication I got this morning has eased the pain somewhat, but I'm so tired. Would you get me a blueberry yogurt from the fridge?"

I obliged, then returned to the front door to say goodbye to the last-minute caregiver friend. Dad shuffled down the hall and I heard the bathroom door close.

The container of yogurt was half eaten on the table, which gave me pause. Dad rarely left food uneaten, and the silence in the house made me move quickly.

I found him sitting on the edge of the bed trying to lie down. "Can you help me? It's so painful to move. Lift my feet."

He drew a sharp breath as he positioned himself on his right side, and he asked for another pillow. I placed a comforter over him, knowing not to cover his feet. I kissed him on the forehead and smoothed what little hair he had back from his face.

A knock on the door pulled me from the room. A blast of icy winter air entered as I opened it to next-door neighbors, Terry and Charlene, who'd come to help me move Dad's favorite recliner from the basement family room to the living room.

We hadn't even greeted each other when a heavy thud came from the bedroom.

The darkness in the bedroom matched the grip on my chest wall. Dad was lying face down on the floor between the bed and the dresser with only inches on either side of him. I straddled his body to feel for a pulse in his neck. I couldn't find one, but I wasn't a trained medical professional.

Charlene's command cut through my indecision. "Call 911."

I raced down the hall, willing my head to stay calm and rehearsing what I would have to say. It seemed like only seconds when the knock on the door thundered.

"I only live down the road, where is he?" said the emergency medical technician, and I pointed toward the bedroom.

The EMT told me that he would need help. "You take his feet, and I will lift under his shoulders. We need to get him on his back. On the count of three."

In three moves we had Dad on his back, on the floor at the foot of the bed. He weighed nearly two hundred pounds. It never occurred to me that I had the power to do such a thing with my tiny frame. I noticed Dad was wearing a pair of his old, tattered jeans, the hems fraying against his bare feet. His T-shirt was thin and spotted. The EMT looked at me, the sadness registering all over his face. He said, "I don't think he will come back this time."

Two more EMTs arrived, bringing the cold snowy air with them all the way to Dad's bedroom, where they began chest compressions and mouth-to-mouth resuscitation. My brain kicked into gear. The Five

Wishes®! And Dad's advance directive! I ran and grabbed the envelope containing the documents that was attached to the refrigerator.

"These are Dad's wishes; he doesn't want to be resuscitated," I said, handing the document over.

I was shocked at how quickly the EMT scanned two documents that held so much emotional energy. "We can't use these. They're years old."

My head was screaming. Dad doesn't want this. He doesn't want this. I said I would protect him. Suddenly, it was as if Mom was standing behind me, her hands resting gently on my shoulders. I quieted. I knew what I needed to do.

The phone number for the hospital was pasted above the ugly mustard-colored wall phone. I spoke each number aloud as I pushed the corresponding button to help calm my breathing, so I'd be able to speak.

When the switchboard picked up, I asked for the transitional care unit. It was answered immediately and, with a sureness I didn't entirely feel, I said, "This is Yvonne Caputo. My father was just released from the unit. There is a DNR on his chart. Please get it to the emergency room. He's being brought in."

By the time I walked back to the bedroom, a call had come through to the EMT working on Dad. The emergency room doctor had given them permission to stop working. I was told it wouldn't be long. I lay down on the floor, on my side, and stretched along the warmth of my father's body. Then I placed my left arm over his chest. My mouth was near his ear.

"Dad, I love you. It's okay for you to go. I know that you want to be with Mom."

I then recited the prayer that had been the family glue, "Our father, who art in heaven, hallowed be thy name . . ."

As I was finishing the prayer, the phone rang. I got up and went into the kitchen to answer it. My brother was on the other end. As I started to explain the night's events, the EMT came into the kitchen. The tender look on his face said it all. It was over.

Dad was placed on a gurney and taken out of his beloved home. As he was being placed in the ambulance, the light from the vehicle's open doors illuminated Dad's face. Gone were the gray, the strain, and the pain. All had been replaced by a warm, sweet smile. I stood beside the ambulance, and I was immersed in opposing feelings. One was overwhelming grief, the other was an equally potent sacred joy.

"Yvonne, I want to be carried out of my home feet first," Dad had said to me that day on his hospital bed.

The snow that I loved so much was falling in big chunky flakes. Lifting my face to the inky sky, I was infused with a sense of triumph. I punched the crisp, cold air with my fists as I screamed into the night, "Yes!"

The EMTs looked at me as if I had lost every one of my marbles.

"My father's wish was to be carried out of his beloved home feet first, and that's exactly what you have done. What we have done." Dad and I had taken this journey together.

I handed my car keys to Charlene and asked her to drive it to the hospital. An EMT helped me onto the passenger seat in the ambulance. The only sound on the ride to the hospital was from the windshield wipers' *slip, slap, slip, slap* across the wet glass. My eyes saw the road ahead, but my head was blank.

When we arrived, I was jolted by the cold glare of the institution's bright lights. The doctor was waiting as I was lead through the door. He spread his arms wide, beckoning me to step in for a hug. He leaned down and spoke softly in my ear. "I knew your dad pretty well. He has gone the way he wanted to."

His reassurance equaled mine, and I turned as Dad's body—not Dad, but Dad's body—was wheeled into the room. He was where his beliefs told him he would be, with Mom.

And then all I wanted was the safety of my car and to be absolutely alone. I couldn't bear the sound of one more voice. I opened the car door and started the engine, its familiarity suddenly unfamiliar. Automatic pilot took me down streets, stopping at red lights, making turns, and climbing the hills, the slush beneath my wheels the only sound.

When I pulled into the driveway and saw the light from the ugly green front door bouncing off the sparkling snow, I broke. It should have said to me "welcome," but it didn't. I turned the key in the lock, pushing at the door's stickiness. The solitude I had so desperately wanted at the hospital now cloyed my skin like the humidity of a hot summer day. I had trouble breathing.

Dad wasn't here, and he would never be here again. I wanted to cry but couldn't. I wanted to be close to his aliveness, so I went into his bedroom and pulled back the covers. I crawled in, still in my jeans and sweater, wrapping the blankets around me, leaving my feet uncovered. Several tears slid from the corner of my eyes on to the pillow that still had the scent of him. Blessed reprieve enveloped me. Sleep came instantly.

20

Amazing Grace

*M*y brother arrived from Kentucky, and my sister from Wisconsin. Both pummeled me with questions about Dad's death. I knew that details were important to them. Both had spent their careers in hospitals—my brother as a pathologist, my sister as a nurse—so the specifics of Dad's death would help them to process this awful, life-altering event.

Both my siblings had spoken to Dad the day before he'd passed and, they told me they were glad that I'd been there. But they wanted to know what made me turn around and drive all the way back the day after I'd just left.

"He asked me. He said he was scared. He'd never said anything like that before, and wild horses wouldn't have kept me from coming."

They said they were relieved Dad didn't die alone.

We called the church and arranged to meet with the priest the following morning. As we sat in his office, Father Gramata asked, "What exactly do you want the funeral mass to look like?"

My sister and brother looked at each other, their faces windows onto all their unanswered questions. "Well, I guess, whatever is standard," my brother replied.

"I know exactly what Dad wanted," I said. "He told me as a part of a process I went through with him, and the results are written down in a document called the Five Wishes."

I went on to list that he wanted a High Mass, and he wanted Kirk to sing the "Lord's Prayer," the "Ave Maria," and "Amazing Grace." He wanted me to sing—I told them I could do that with Kirk on "Amazing Grace." I explained that Dad didn't have a preference for what scripture was used, that he'd said that we could decide.

"It would be nice to get other family members involved," my brother said. He went on to speak about the roles the grandchildren could have and how some, along with grand nephews, could be pall-bearers.

My sister added that she'd like to read some scripture as well.

Remembering something else from the Five Wishes®, I said to the priest, "Father, Dad did not want congregants to stand up and share memories." I lowered my tone, mimicking Dad's deep, resonant voice, "I don't want people standing up and talking about me. If they hadn't said it to my face, then I'm damned sure I don't want them saying it during the service."

The atmosphere in the room shattered like an icicle hitting concrete. Laughter filled all the tight spaces. Dad might be gone, but his sarcasm, rooted in truth and humor, remained. Dad had just gotten something else he would have wanted—we were laughing with him. While we were planning his funeral, the last laugh was from him.

Seriousness returned as we moved on with the importance of what we were planning. This was to be our father's last Mass. This would say to all of those gathered: we are honoring this man, who he was, what he meant to us, and what he believed.

In letters Dad had written to Teddy (Mom) when he was stationed overseas during WWII, he often mentioned what it meant to him to be at Mass. Reading between the lines, it was what sustained him through the horror of the war. He wanted to go to confession so that he could receive communion, particularly if he was slated to go out on a bombing mission. Knowing full well that he might die on the mission, he wanted to be in a state of grace. He believed that would guarantee him a place in heaven.

Dad's grandchildren, grandnephews, and his niece arrived in the following days. The night before the funeral, we gathered at the funeral home to say our last goodbyes. We stood around the open casket as Father Gramata said the ritual prayers of burial, "Come to me all you who are labored and are over-burdened and I will give you rest..."

The reality of Dad's death permeated the room, but the soft, sweet smile on his face mirrored the spoken words.

The following morning, we were seated together as a family as the Mass began. The pall-bearers came and took their place across the aisle from us. The casket, covered with an ivory pall with a large plain golden cross, rested at the front of the church. Father Gramata sprinkled holy water on the casket to remind us of Dad's baptism those many years ago, and he swung the incense-laden censer to honor Dad's body, and to remind us of our prayers for Dad going to heaven.

The ritual we knew so well—even though it was Dad's funeral— was soothing. Standing, genuflecting, kneeling at the appropriate times, all of it a reminder of the deep faith that kept Dad going in the best and worst of times.

My sister and my niece read their chosen scriptures with wondrous clarity. Each word a sacred gift to the man they so respected and adored.

At the recitation of the "Lord's Prayer," everyone in the family pew reached for the hand of the person standing on either side. We were that solid family unit honoring the man who had helped to make us all possible.

Kirk and I walked to the front of the church to sing "Amazing Grace." I should have been scared out of my shoes, but something quietly took over. I was wrapped in a blanket of calm and purpose. I wasn't going to let Dad down.

When the Mass ended, we stepped into the aisle to follow the casket. The organist started to play the "Air Force Hymn," and my sister and I began to sing, "Off we go into the wild blue yonder, climbing high into the sun..."

Because of Dad's request for that hymn—revealed as part of his five wishes—my brother had reached out to the local American Legion, and the graveside ended with the playing of "Taps" and a twenty-one-gun salute.

21

Onward: Fear Not

*M*y place of work gave five days of bereavement leave after the death of a parent. I knew of other companies that were less generous, including some that gave nothing. I made good use of those five days. We found someone to look after Dad's house, to check on it daily given Meadville was in the dead of winter. The funeral arrangements were completed, and the bill settled. We children and the grandchildren went through the house and took mementos that provided much needed memories of the two beautiful souls we had lost.

But I hadn't taken nearly enough time for me. The pace hadn't slowed. I hadn't had time to process. I wondered how on earth was I going to be able to put one foot in front of the other, let alone be productive at work. I was due back the following day.

And yet life goes on.

And it did.

Steps and setbacks take place for us all. We move on. We slow, then we pick up. We do what has to be done. It's called life.

We have all kinds of expressions for living that refer to not dying: we cheat death, come close to it, have a brush with it. For some—after diagnosis of a terminal illness—they live on what some say is borrowed time. Others, who defy the prognoses, live in a survivorship. Perhaps we all live in a version of a suspended death since we will all die.

In fairy tales, fairy godmothers appear at the birth of children and grant wishes and bestow goodness and blessings. In real life, we do as much with congratulations, cards, gifts, and flowers for the newborns who arrive in the families of our loved ones. There is so much chatter about what will come during that child's lifetime. There is so much promise. There is happiness, and seemingly no fear. There is talk about what that child needs for their journey.

But when that child who has turned into an adult and nears the end of a natural life, the conversations about what that person needs are absent.

In scripture, the phrase "fear not" is a common one. Don't be scared. It's okay. Yet we have not quite mastered this when it comes to end-of-life conversations, and the respect they generate when they take place well before the end of life.

Going through advance directive and the Five Wishes® processes with Dad helped me see that our journey is worth all the challenges because life is joy. "Fear not" I hear. Aging is a privilege. And connection is a gift.

22

My Five Wishes

*N*one of us can dictate how others must grieve when we leave. But perhaps, with the Five Wishes® in hand, they can make decisions with the same resolve and experience the peace that I did when Dad's life came to an end.

That sense of the wonder of doing the Five Wishes® with Dad has never left me. But doing my own Five Wishes®? I, like many others, can make procrastination a fine art. My will and attorney-prepared advance directive are in the fireproof box in a closet. Our children know where to find them.

Since coping has been a lifelong pursuit for me and helping others to cope has been my profession, I want the loved ones I leave behind to be able to cope too. I believe in my heart that the Five Wishes® will help them cope more successfully with my death.

A plethora of emotions flooded me each time I started—many of the views of those readers of *Flying With Dad* are echoed by me. I resisted, convincing myself I didn't want to write the answers but type them... That helped me delay for a few weeks.

A monologue like this would take place in my mind: Intellectually, I know I'm going to die, but my heart has a little bit of trouble catching up with that idea. I am seventy-five years young, and I'm healthy. I've lived a full, sometimes depressing but more often exhilarating, life. I have no problem saying that I want more. I am not ready to call it quits, so it's too soon to do my own Five Wishes® exercise.

Then I'd remind myself that this was not what the Five Wishes® is about. I pushed on and, regardless of my previous role of advocate and educator, I sometimes felt anxious and fearful.

Mom's experience when she was younger—leaving her body, not wanting to come back—was one that challenges even the deepest of faith. I believe in an afterlife, and her experience validated that for me.

I vacillated between emotional and intellectual. I compromised with a brand of pragmatic. And I discovered that Aging with Dignity provides a way to complete the Five Wishes® document online. The PDF can be saved and updated for up to a year.

Consider The Five Wishes®

When anyone works on their Five Wishes®, they will need to think about who they will choose as their health care agent. For me, the word *trust* came to the forefront. The health care agent or agents would need to be people I trusted to make decisions on my behalf, even if they didn't understand why I had requested or wished certain things.

I know this is not always possible within some families. What an individual wants may go against the beliefs and interests of other family members. Conflict and strife is another reason that looking outside the family may be necessary. Health care agents can be a friend, a church member, or an attorney.

Those attempting to complete their Five Wishes®, or assisting someone in completing theirs, must, I believe, have a global view of the fact that life events have led to certain wishes. For example, my own wishes have been informed by my mom's lack of mobility in her last five years. And there needs to be a comfort level with the instructions, so the administrative portion does not overshadow the deep and sacred task of the wishes themselves.

I created my Five Wishes® alone. I knew that my advocates were trusted and would honour my wishes. But had I had assistance, I would want that person to understand my reasons for my wishes, and as a person helping someone prepare theirs—as I did with Dad—I needed to understand and respect why he made his. It wasn't a time for debate.

Because I have worked in environments that serve the elderly, I have also been influenced by things I've witnessed for others in care. I don't fear being in a nursing home—I'd welcome one that is carefully chosen. But I do fear being immobile. One of the experiences that feeds this involves a resident at Frederick Living. He had a large walker with an insert to step into and rolling wheels to scoot. For months, I watched the resident going up and down halls—smiling to beat the band most of the time. He was moving. But a change in state rules meant that, sadly, his inability to get in and out of his walker on his own meant it was now classified as a restraint. He could no longer legally use the walker, and his quality of life immediately plummeted. I never saw him in the halls again.

Memories and experiences like this one of mine will influence each person's desires for their end of life. Though we can't know everything, what's happened in our lives will inform our decisions.

For me, as I pushed on, putting my wishes on paper was a discomfiting and clear acknowledgement of the reality of my death. It signalled acceptance of my lack of control over the eventuality. Signing my Five Wishes® and having two special people witness my signature felt like a victory. Making copies and addressing envelopes to my children, my doctor, and my attorney—and then mailing them—marked a sobering finish.

On the other side, my heart was filled with the joy of accomplishment. I knew that what I had done would help those closest to me during a time that will be filled with sorrow.

Saying I love them is no longer a whisper or a shout into the air, it's something they can hold in their hands. It's the warm all-encompassing embrace I hope they'll remember for the rest of their lives.

I believe in science and the concept that energy cannot be destroyed. It is energy that allows my body to transform food into movement, and it is energy that is released through the heat escaping from my body. It is energy's electrical impulses that allow my brain to function and to send messages throughout me.

When I die, that energy will go somewhere else in some way. How it works doesn't really matter to me because I believe strongly in an afterlife. I'm ready to join those who have gone before. I'm blessed to have had a mom who had a near-death experience to help me believe in the serenity that will come. Her experience helped me. I believe that my spirit will live on long after my body is gone.

Completing my Five Wishes® and discussing them with loved ones turned out not to be difficult. Peter and Kate had similar questions and responses, and a few unique too.

Peter wanted to know if my wishes would change if I could move with a walker or a wheelchair. He asked whether intubation would be okay with me if my illness were acute rather than an end-of-life palliative stage. And he said he just new Dan Fogelberg would be on the list of music I wanted to play at my memorial service. He noted the absence of "being a parent" on the list of things for which I wanted to be remembered.

Kate needed to dig into more specifics around how I—and we—would know whether I still had all my mental faculties, and how we'd know when I was past my arbitrary cut-off point. While she and I had discussed some of these issues in the past, she said it was helpful to have it in writing.

NOT EVERYONE SHARES MY BELIEFS. I AM NOT EVERYONE, I AM ME. OUR individuality allows us to experience life's lessons at different stages and to form unique opinions which, combined, create a diverse world. We are all bridge builders. We are all seekers of the truth. And we are all, as Ram Dass says, "Walking each other home."

As you age with dignity, as you pursue your interests, and fulfill promises to yourself, as you serve others and advocate for them, and while you consider the impact of the Five Wishes®, or discussion of something similar, may you:

Feel relief: now that the subject has been raised, you can now go there.

Be inspired: to speak about the topic with loved ones and have it be okay for all.

Sense movement: that eases the seemingly difficult something by illustrating the incredible release the outcome offers.

Experience peace: knowing that taking action toward the Five Wishes® initiative can bring just that... peace.

Celebrate life as a joyful journey. Be confident that the courage to face doing the Five Wishes® to assist a loved one, or doing it for yourself, is an act of unconditional love and profound respect. To actively provide someone you love with the most passionate send-off for the next part of their journey enhances your own time left upon this planet. And when it is done for you, it enriches the lives of those involved in honoring your wishes.

Accept and run with the challenge—do something for your family or loved ones that makes dying easier.

And may you remember:

Talking about death and dying, particularly your own, is okay. It doesn't mean you are wishing to go right now or that you're wishing someone else would.

Talking about it doesn't mean that the listener is trying to push the loved one into wanting to die. It means that thought can go into what is precious and sacred to each of us and, when the time comes, that which is precious and sacred is honored.

Talking about it simplifies and clarifies the tasks that are put upon us and healthcare professionals when the time is emotionally charged, and people are physically tasked with duties.

It is a set of intimate directives. A difficult topic to broach, yet, once raised, a tremendous act of love and respect. Once the list is made, relationships shift to a higher level, life is lighter, the knowing more about the person (including yourself) sheds light on existing experiences, turning that knowingness into, well, sparks of energetic gifting... sparkles, if you like.

Let's say you discover one of a friend's wishes is to be surrounded by a specific flower or color... well, that is information you have in the here and now to bring that into someone's life prior to the send-off to their next journey.

Going through the process of the Five Wishes® informs, it brings life to life, and life to death.

As I write this, it's been more than eleven years since Dad's passing and the fulfillment of his Five Wishes®. The grieving that I have done for him is vastly different from what I experienced when losing my brother and my mother. Both of those were heart-wrenching for months into years. With Mark, the agony centered around all that was unfinished in his young and promising life. He didn't live long enough to accomplish his dreams, nor did I get to walk along with him as he might have grown and changed.

With Mom, her death happened in the sterile, clinical, and antiseptic hospital. She wasn't in her own bed in her home with the husband that she cherished. Our final conversation was her screaming for me to take her home. I now know her screaming wasn't formed in anger, but in terror. She didn't know where she was, or why she was there.

When I think about that call, the screams come rushing back into my head, and I regret not being able to soothe her in the way she so justly deserved. That feeling is somewhat relieved in that, when I saw her for the first time in the funeral home, she too had a soft, sweet smile on her face. She was where she wanted to be.

With Dad, I experienced something brand new. My grieving centered on missing him. As I worked on this book, I wanted to be able to call him and ask, "So you said this about that, tell me more." I still want that. I miss his all-consuming hugs; the ones that said, "Give it time and it will all be okay."

With Dad, there has never been heart-wrenching sorrow. Instead, there is an ever-recurring feeling of joy, a sacred joy.

It was as if we were walking along a flat trail though a sun-drenched meadow, a row of strong sturdy oaks on our right and bleached waving grain on our left. We were hand in hand, sharing memories and laughter. We both knew that, when we came to the end of the trail, I would have to let go of his hand and watch him walk into the unknown.

It was done, and it was good, so very, very good. And I want that for you too.

May this book start conversations that become the magic of legacy.

Passing the Five Wishes On

I finished addressing the last of the three large white envelopes, walked out the side door along the path of gray and red pavers and down the driveway, the crunching gravel sounding… different somehow. Reaching the black mailbox that stood on the grassy edge at the side of the road, I pulled the handle and placed the stamped envelopes inside. For a moment, I peered into the box, thinking how strange that such thin white envelopes could contain such enormity. Satisfaction rose from my feet up to the top of my head as I closed the door and lifted the red flag that would tell the carrier there was mail to pick up. They'd be traveling many miles, these envelopes: one to the east coast and two to the west coast. Soon these envelopes would be in the hands of each of my three children.

Inside each envelope was a copy of my Five Wishes®. The documents would formalize the many discussions that I'd had with my adult children about what I wanted when the end came, topics and talks that no longer floated off into the air. My wishes for my end of life would have remained just that—fairy-tale wishes—unless I had written them down, documented and signed and witnessed. They were still my wishes, but now they enjoyed the full force of the law. And my children, or my husband, wouldn't find themselves powerless to implement my wishes because I hadn't gone to the trouble of writing down exactly what I wanted.

I've lost count of the number of conversations I've had with friends, family, and colleagues who don't think they need to write down their end-of-life wishes because they've *talked* to their loved ones.

MY DAUGHTER DEBORAH LIVES IN A SMALL APARTMENT COMPLEX IN beautiful sunny southern California. A few doors down from her was a darling bungalow, a powder blue 1969 Mustang parked in the drive. Deborah would see Louise, the spritely ninety-two-year-old owner who'd lived there for the better part of her life, driving the car, often returning with groceries, looking remarkably well despite her age. Deborah and Louise became friends.

Predictably, considering her age, Louise's health began to deteriorate, and Deborah assisted by purchasing groceries for her. They also set up a communication system so Deborah would know if Louise needed assistance. Deborah would tuck the daily newspaper in the mail slot in the door, leaving it half-way out and visible from the outside. If all was well with Louise, she'd grab the paper and the empty mail slot was the signal that all was well.

Many times, Louise had told Deborah that she wanted to die in her own home. She also made it clear she was ready to go—and any day would be soon enough.

Soon Deborah began to worry about Louise's welfare. The newspaper would be gone each day, but when she used the key Louise had given her to let herself in, she began to notice the smell of urine. The living room and the kitchen were not as neat and tidy as they had been. At each visit, the smell and disarray became increasingly worse. Deborah was a neighbor, and she didn't feel the issues were hers to address. Louise's next of kin and legal caretaker was a niece, Jean, that lived in another state.

Because of my experience working with the elderly, Deborah and I had talked about options that might be available for Louise. The most important was to make sure Jean knew what was going on and to ask her to come and assist.

"Does Louise have an advance directive?" I asked Deborah on one of our calls.

"I don't honestly know. But I'll talk to Jean to see what she knows."

Then Deborah's big white envelope arrived, and Deborah called.

"I'm so glad you've sent this to me." I could hear the energy sparking all the way from California to Pennsylvania. I got myself prepared to discuss the details I'd written in my Five Wishes® document with my daughter, but Deborah had other ideas altogether.

"I'm going to order the Five Wishes document and get it express shipped for Jean and Louise." Deborah filled me in with the latest. Jean had come, and together with Deborah they entered Louise's home. Louise had lost the ability to get herself to the bathroom and the living room sofa was drenched and reeking. The kitchen was piled high with dirty dishes. Jean regretted not traveling to see her aunt sooner, and Deborah regretted not calling Jean sooner.

Once the home and Louise were cleaned up and there were at least temporary home supports in place, Jean and Deborah introduced the Five Wishes® to Louise and took her through the booklet step by step. Louise seemed non-plussed about the questions, like she was being asked what her favorite color was or whether she preferred brown or white rice. But the purpose of the Five Wishes® was completed. Louise had officially appointed Jean as her health care agent. And Jean had all of the information and legal backing she needed to make decisions on her aunt's behalf.

My heart was full of compassion for Jean and Louise. The Five Wishes® had guided them through one of life's toughest conversations. Their upcoming journey together had become so much easier to navigate. Although their road might not necessarily be easier, there was peace of mind from having the map in hand.

My heart was full of pride for my daughter. Deborah told me she'd cried when she'd opened her white envelope and read my Five Wishes®—she had to face the fact that someday death would come to me. At the same time, she felt a burden had lifted. She now had a step-by-step recipe that would guide her, along with Peter and Kate, my other two children, in the decisions that would have to be made when my time came.

As uncomfortable as it might have been for her, she took her newfound knowledge, and she orchestrated a discussion between two others. She had taken the gift that I had received from my father, that I had then given to her, and she passed it on.

24

Schooling And Skinny Skis

*E*very time I step out of my skinny cross-country skis and feel the gravel under the soles of my boots, it's another question mark. Is this going to be my last ski of the season? Sliding my glove the full length of the base of each ski and watching muddy slush slop to the ground, I know the snow could all be gone tomorrow. Where I live, snow coverage is somewhat iffy. Lifting the hatchback on my little red car and sliding my skis in, the thought that this might have been the final outing of the season leaves a dry taste in my mouth. I'd be happy to have snow from the beginning of November until late March. Or longer.

When I express my love of the cold, and the covering of white all around me, people sometimes look at me suspiciously, the crinkles around their eyes questioning my sanity. I just smile. Being alone in the woods, feeling the push then slide of my skis on the trails, fills me with awe over the magic of being alive.

Some days, the conditions make it easy—soft, dry snow, deep enough to cover roots and stones but not so deep that I must push too hard, and the gliding is a dream. Sometimes I meet a fox or deer in the woods. If I stay still, they're willing to share the space with me. Hawks, or a rare sighting of a bald eagle, remind me to look up and out into the great resource we call the sky.

Some days, the conditions are challenging. Melting snow means avoiding puddles or bare spots. Icy days mean I may struggle to stay upright. Deep snow makes my heart pound with the exertion that it takes to carve my own path. The worst skiing happens when soft, dry snow is laying on the wet snow underneath. Big knobs of snow freeze to the bottom of the ski, making pushing forward impossible. On those days, I mutter under my breath as I take off my skis, scrape the snow off the bottom, then throw the skis over my shoulder for a disappointing trudge back to my car.

Whatever the conditions, the snow always beckons. I don't always know what conditions will greet me, and I head out as often as I can anyway. Just like Mary's message in the song playing on the radio after I'd accompanied her body out of the home. Just like I didn't know how Dad was going to react to the Five Wishes® and I brought it up anyway.

In the years since that first skiing adventure, I've skied in all kinds of weather and conditions. I have cut a trail through deep snow, plodding by bringing the ski up and then pushing it back down. Up and down, up and down, with each stroke making my heart pound and my breath labored. I exerted all that effort because I knew, on the way back, I would get to stride and glide.

There is a lot of work to cross-country skiing and—and, not but—it provides a lot of pleasure. Each time I'm on my skis, it requires a little bit of adjustment. There is generally some good and some bad, but there is always the joy of the rhythm and the glide, and being out in the white, glorious world. Just like the relationship between me and my father.

Deep down, I knew he loved me to pieces, but we didn't ever seem to find that place of ease with each other. That is, until he began to tell me his WWII stories, and I began to listen deeply and write them down. It took until my early sixties, but the shift in our relationship that I'd been seeking for so long began to materialize. Through my inquiries and his responses, he opened up to me in ways that had never been possible before.

Both Dad and skiing required me to put one foot in front of the other. Sometimes the steps were easy, and sometimes they were exhausting. There was excruciating cold and sublime warmth. There was slush and gray and unbelievable pristine white. There was overwhelming sorrow and great joy. I had to learn to put aside my hesitancy, to do something hard, resulting in learning to do something beautiful. A divine paradox. I wouldn't have had either any other way.

Years after Dad's death, the paradox holds true. The grief process has been so vastly different than it had been with Mom or my brother. Yes, his death was awful, like having to take off my skis and slog out of the woods but, at the same time, it was breathtakingly beautiful, a glorious and sacred event. I will always be soothed by how and why it happened in the way that it did.

The result was that, on the day he died, I was able to participate in his going. I was able to help orchestrate it so that it happened in exactly the way he wanted it to. We had crossed the finish line—his finish line —together in a joyful and triumphant success.

25

Hey, Yvonne! Tell Me More

*W*hile each person is unique in their situations, experiences, understandings, obstacles, personalities, and beliefs, the responses I received to *Flying With Dad* reflected the novelty of this concept. "I want to know more. I know this is important." And "This is uncomfortable and unfamiliar," and "This scares the hell out of me." I began to purposely initiate conversations with people around the topic of end-of-life conversations, dying with dignity, and the Five Wishes®. Here's what I heard:

- When are we too young to complete the Five Wishes®?
- How is it possible to make a decision right now?
- How much does it cost?
- Do I need an attorney?
- Dying is unthinkable, let alone being something to talk about.
- If I talk about death by doing the Five Wishes®, I'm worried it could make death happen sooner.
- How do I know what to say in raising the subject with a loved one?

- What if things change? Can it be updated?
- I'm sure my wishes are already known by loved ones, so why write them down?
- Who would be prepared to take on the role of a health care agent—strong enough to stand up to medical professionals and others?
- How do I handle family resistance?

By being curious, the people asking these questions were inviting themselves to grow. They were saying, "Yvonne, you touched on this in your first book… help me gain a better understanding of what's involved with end-of-life conversations. Get me thinking, Yvonne. Motivate me to do for myself and my loved ones what you did for your dad."

Some acknowledged there would be challenges, but said:

- It would be an amazing Christmas gift, or anytime gift, for an elder in their family—maybe for themselves too.
- There is clarity with this plan: four surviving children all with different personalities and views will be brought together by such a document.
- It would be an honor to be a health care advocate—what a service and a wonderful way to learn more about a loved one.
- What a fantastic way to lessen the burden on others; to take the steps to relieve family of stressful decisions and tasks.

I'm interested in sharing my story as a way to help others build the bridge between no end-of-life conversation and seeing the possibility of doing the Five Wishes®. To get people thinking. For them to hear the anecdotes and witness my journey as a health care agent, and an originator of my own wishes.

If You Enjoyed Dying With Dad

Acknowledgments

Writing a book is a solitary process. However, for a book to be a solid piece of work, it has to have the help and guidance of others.

First and foremost, I have to acknowledge Zenta Benner. She was the national health administrator at Frederick Mennonite Community, the retirement community where I was vice president of human resources. Zenta is the one who handed me the precious document called the Five Wishes®. She was dedicated and attuned to the residents we served.

The community, now known as Frederick Living, was my home away from home for seventeen years. It was there that I met and fell in love with those residents who were sharing their final years with me and the rest of the staff. By getting to know some of them and observing others, I began to understand what growing old gracefully really meant. I also began to see the other side of that coin. The faces surrounding me were either etched with sadness and foreboding or lit with the joy of a life well-lived.

Those who trusted me with their willingness to talk about wanting to go demonstrated a faith in me that allowed me to sit back and listen... to their despondence over having no one else around, to their feelings of loss in no longer having a purpose or the ability to do the things they loved, to their readiness to go and join their loved ones, or to just go.

I am grateful to my brother Michael and my sister Connie. Michael let me know when it came to caring for the emotional health of our parents that he trusted me to do what I thought needed to be done. Connie told me that she was thankful I was with Dad on his final journey.

As I was writing *Dying with Dad*, I interviewed several people about doing the Five Wishes® process with their loved ones. Their input confirmed what makes these tough talks difficult, but I like to think I helped them see what is possible, to think differently about the process and its importance. Thank you, C.A. Gibbs, Elizabeth Burnham, Richard Wagner, and Molly Lord.

Many thanks to my editor and publisher, Boni Wagner-Stafford, at Ingenium Books. She is a storyteller's storyteller. She has taken my thoughts, sentences, and paragraphs and with a little nudge here and a little nudge there, helped me create a story that comes sliding off the page and into the arms of my readers.

My daughter Deborah and my stepchildren Peter and Kate have been wonderful as I have gone through the process of doing my own Five Wishes®. They were open to the conversations and never shied away from hearing the hard things. They affirmed it was so much easier to know what I wanted rather than having to guess at the time of my death.

To Jim Towey, for having created the Five Wishes®. It became the powerful tool I needed to honor my dad. It guided me to ask all the questions that needed to be answered about how my dad wanted his end to be, and in the end, I was able to be the spokesperson my father needed.

Ed Towey, the Vice President for Advocacy for Aging with Dignity read and provided notes on the parts about the origins of the Five Wishes®.

My husband Kirk has been my continual onsite cheerleader. He reads me like a book and knows exactly when I need a listening ear, or a compliment, or a little push. Mostly he keeps telling me that I am doing the right things and that all of it will pay off. So far, he's been right.

Finally, to the right of my computer monitor is a picture of my parents, Mike and Teddy Caputo, shortly after their marriage. He is in his USAAF uniform and she is wearing his navigator's pin. They are young, in love, smiling, and radiant. I'm grateful for the wonderful parents they were. This book is a testament to their belief in me.

Bibliography

"10 Life Lessons Learned from Hospice Patients." Memorial Health Blog, April 1, 2016. https://web.archive.org/web/20220120182243/https://blog.memorial.health/10-life-lessons-learned-hospice-patients/

"5 Wishes Living Will Document: Printable 5 Wishes Form." Samaritan. Samaritan, April 27, 2020. https://web.archive.org/web/20220120182340/https://samaritannj.org/resources/5-wishes-living-will-documents/

Adair, Bill. "Full of Faith, Full of Desire." *Tampa Bay Times*. February 10, 2002. https://web.archive.org/web/20220120204203/https://www.tampabay.com/archive/2002/02/10/full-of-faith-full-of-desire/

Adair, Bill. "Towey's Zeal Bothers Critics." *Tampa Bay Times*. February 2, 2002. https://web.archive.org/web/20220120204402/https://www.tampabay.com/archive/2002/02/02/towey-s-zeal-bothers-critics

Andreae, Christine. *When Evening Comes: The Education of a Hospice Volunteer*. New York, NY: St. Martin's Press, 2000

Beck, Julie. "Why Humans Care for the Bodies of the Dead." The Atlantic. Atlantic Media Company, November 12, 2015. https://web.

archive.org/web/20210423001602/https://www.theatlantic.com/health/archive/2015/11/why-humans-care-for-the-bodies-of-the-dead/415425/

Caputo, Yvonne. Ed Towey of Five Wishes Center, Florida. Personal, September 23, 2021

Cherry, Kendra. "How the Color Blue Impacts Moods, Feelings, and Behaviors." Verywell Mind. Verywell Mind, April 8, 2018. https://web.archive.org/web/20211229205743/https://www.verywellmind.com/the-color-psychology-of-blue-2795815

"Color Symbolism." Wikipedia. Wikimedia Foundation. Last modified September 13, 2006. https://web.archive.org/web/20211216202515/https://en.wikipedia.org/wiki/Color_symbolism

Crossroads Hospice Charitable Foundation. "Understanding Hospice Volunteering." Crossroads Hospice Charitable Foundation. Crossroads Hospice Charitable Foundation, September 25, 2015. https://web.archive.org/web/20210407200107/https://crhcf.org/insights/understanding-hospice-volunteering/

"Death Odor Removal and Cleanup." Aftermath Services | Crime Scene Clean Up & Death Cleanup Professionals, June 21, 2018. https://web.archive.org/web/20210422203836/https://www.aftermath.com/services/specialty-services/odor-removal

"Five Wishes for Individuals and Families." Your Living Will and Advance Directive | Five Wishes For You, June 20, 2018. https://web.archive.org/web/20211231160755/https://fivewishes.org/five-wishes/individuals-families/individuals-and-families

"Five Wishes." Wikipedia. Wikimedia Foundation. Last modified December 29, 2021. https://web.archive.org/web/20211103220334/https://en.wikipedia.org/wiki/Five_Wishes

"Healthcare Providers." Five Wishes for Healthcare Organizations and Providers. Five Wishes, June 18, 2018. https://web.archive.org/web/20220120205357/https://fivewishes.org/five-wishes/health-care-systems

"Home Funeral History." NATIONAL HOME FUNERAL

ALLIANCE. NATIONAL HOME FUNERAL ALLIANCE, July 8, 2018. https://web.archive.org/web/20210818231328/https://www. homefuneralalliance.org/home-funeral-history.html

Horst, Glen R. Care of the body after death. Canadian Virtual Hospice, June 4, 2015. https://web.archive.org/web/20210814132847/ https://www.virtualhospice.ca/en_US/Main+Site+Navigation/ Home/Topics/Topics/Final+Days/Care+of+the+Body+ After+Death.aspx

"HR & Business Professionals." Five Wishes for HR Professionals. Five Wishes, June 18, 2018. https://web.archive.org/web/ 20210813102243/https://fivewishes.org/five-wishes/businesses/five-wishes-in-your-business/hr-and-business-professionals

"Jim Towey." Wikipedia. Wikimedia Foundation. Last modified August 20, 2021. https://web.archive.org/web/20211204221856/ https://en.wikipedia.org/wiki/Jim_Towey

Key, Joel. "The Road Less Travelled Summary (M. Scott Peck)." Bloomsoup, March 27, 2020. https://web.archive.org/web/ 20220120205535/https://bloomsoup.com/the-road-less-travelled-m-scott-peck/

Lynch, Craig O. *The Hospice Volunteer Handbook: Volume One - The Friendly Visitor (Volume 1)*. 1. Vol. 1. Self-Published, CreateSpace, 2017

Marshall, Jeffrey. "What Happens If I Don't Have an Advance Directive? – Marshall, Parker & Weber." Marshall Parker Weber, October 2, 2018. https://web.archive.org/web/20220120205634/ https://www.paelderlaw.com/estate-planning/what-happens-if-i-dont-have-an-advance-directive/

Nuland, Sherwin B. *How We Die: Reflections on Life's Final Chapter*. New York, NY: Vintage Books, 1995

Owen, Adrian M. *Into the Gray Zone: A Neuroscientist Explores the Border between Life and Death*. New York, NY: Simon & Schuster, 2017

Peck, M. Scott. *The Road Less Traveled: A New Psychology of Love, Traditional Values and Spiritual Growth*. New York, NY: Simon & Schuster, 2003

"Religions - Spiritualism: Spiritualism at a Glance." BBC. BBC, September 22, 2009. https://web.archive.org/web/20211227123329/https://www.bbc.co.uk/religion/religions/spiritualism/ataglance/glance.shtml

"Talking About Death and Dying." Hospice UK. Hospice UK, May 11, 2018. https://web.archive.org/web/20211201183413/https://www.hospiceuk.org/information-and-support/death-and-dying-what-expect/about-death-and-dying

"Top 25 Quotes by M. Scott Peck (of 162): A-Z Quotes." AZ Quotes, August 24, 2014. https://web.archive.org/web/20210822121412/https://www.azquotes.com/author/11465-M_Scott_Peck

"What to Do after Someone Dies." National Institute on Aging. U.S. Department of Health and Human Services, July 28, 2017. https://web.archive.org/web/20220103045038/https://www.nia.nih.gov/health/what-do-after-someone-dies

"Who We Are." Our History & Mission, December 18, 2018. https://web.archive.org/web/20211220170037/https://fivewishes.org/five-wishes/who-we-are/about-us/our-history-and-mission

About the Author

Yvonne Caputo has been a teacher, the head of human resources in a retirement community, a corporate trainer and consultant, and a psychotherapist. She has master's degrees in education and in clinical psychology. Her first book, *Flying with Dad,* is a story about her relationship with her father through his telling of World War II stories. *Dying with Dad* is Yvonne's second book.

She has always been a storyteller. She has used stories to widen the eyes of students, and to soften the pain of clients. It's her stories that result in rave reviews as a presenter and a speaker.

Yvonne lives in Pennsylvania with her best friend (who is also her husband). Together they have three children, three grandchildren, and a labradoodle called Maggie.

Further Reading

*F*ive Wishes also produces a booklet called *Conversation Guide for Individuals and Families*. It contains suggestions on how to start the conversation. It provides step-by-step instruction. It explores who needs to have a copy and why for after the document is complete.

Also by Yvonne Caputo

Flying With Dad:

A Daughter. A Father. And the Hidden Gifts in his Stories from WWII.

yvonnecaputo.com

Other Books to Enjoy from Ingenium Books

Leaving the Safe Harbor:
The Risks and Rewards of Raising a Family on a Boat

tanyahackney.com

Four Fridays with Christina:
Friendship, Death, and Lessons Learned by Letting Go

ingeniumbooks.com / cynthia-barlow

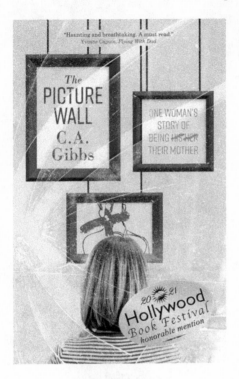

The Picture Wall:
One Woman's Story of Being ~~His~~ ~~Her~~ Their Mother

cagibbs.com

In the Thick of It:
Mastering the Art of Leading from the Middle

gwynteatro.com

The Promise of Psychedelics:
Science Based Hope for Better Mental Health

petersilverstone.com